A basic course in art

Linear and spatial composition. Girl age 17.

Leslie W. Lawley A.T.D

A basic course in art

Lund Humphries · London

Contents

Acknowledgements

I should like to express my indebtedness to the stimulus I received as a student at the Scarborough Summer School in 1957 when I first met the ideas which were being developed by Victor and Wendy Pasmore, Harry Thubron, and Tom Hudson, as the new foundation of art teaching now in use at the Department of Fine Art, Durham University, Newcastle-upon-Tyne, and at Leeds College of Art.

Since that time I have used this approach and have adapted these methods to the needs of boys and girls in different kinds of secondary schools.

In this book I have tried whenever possible to use actual examples of children's work to illustrate the points made. I am grateful to the Governors and Headmaster of Malton Grammar School and to the Headmistress of St Andrew's School for Girls, Malton, Yorkshire, for permission to use some of the children's work for this purpose.

I should like to thank Frank Bowman, lately Senior Lecturer in Art at Scarborough Teachers' Training College, now Principal Lecturer in Art and Crafts at Cheshire County Training College, Crewe, for reading the manuscript and making suggestions; and Jeanne Fletcher for help with the typing.

NOTE.   Of the 36 pages of illustration in this book, plates 1, 3, 5, 9, 11, 13, 14, 16, 18, 20, 21, 26, 27, 28 and 29 have been prepared by the author. They demonstrate typical work that can be expected in the secondary school. The other 21 plates reproduce examples of children's work. The endpaper design is the work of a girl aged 15.

Foreword

by Sir Herbert Read

In the past few years the idea of what is called 'a basic course' in art teaching has been much discussed, and in three or four centres, notably King's College, University of Durham, and the Leeds College of Art, has been put into practice, with astonishing results. The idea is not new – it was the 'backbone' of the Bauhaus system from its very beginning in 1919, when Walter Gropius appointed Johannes Itten to conduct such a course at Weimar. Gropius had met Itten in Vienna in 1918 where he was directing a private school and had been so impressed by his methods of teaching that he decided to make him his chief collaborator. Most of the methods now incorporated in the Basic Course described by Mr Lawley were first evolved experimentally by Professor Itten, but afterwards Klee and Kandinsky were to elaborate these new methods of teaching.

The basic course at the Bauhaus required: (1) the analytical study of raw materials, to learn the range of their expressive possibilities; (2) free composition with such materials, the art we now call 'assemblage', to show how their differences can be reconciled by qualities like rhythm, balance and harmony; and (3) the structural analysis of existing works of art (old masters). Between the foundation of the Bauhaus in 1919 and its closure in 1933 a whole pedagogic system of design was built up on these principles and then suddenly destroyed by evil politicians.

There have been several attempts to restore the system in other countries, notably by Moholy-Nagy who established a New Bauhaus in Chicago in 1937. Indeed, 'the Bauhaus idea' could not be destroyed – it had been a great success and had inspired teachers throughout the world. But it is one thing to inspire teachers and quite another to establish schools of design. It is even more difficult to penetrate schools already established and committed to a traditional method of teaching. But that is what is happening now, on an increasing scale and with indisputable success.

Such a new method is in need of new textbooks, both for the teacher and the student, and this is what Mr Lawley has now provided. It is a severely practical book and all the better for that reason. But it is not a dogmatic book, for as Mr Lawley well realizes, there is a fundamental contradiction between art and dogma. Klee said of his basic course that it was 'a device for achieving clarity'. He warned his students against a new formalism, a new academicism. What the student learns in a basic course is a new language, a language of forms. It is nobody's business to teach him what to say in this new language. Having learned the language, he should then use it to communicate his own vision.

Introduction

For some time it has been clear that certain changes are necessary in art education in secondary schools. Tribute has often been paid to the excellent work done in infant and junior primary schools. This has been achieved mainly on the emotional and intuitive levels through 'free expression' in pattern or imaginative painting. But at the secondary stage there has been a bewildering variety of methods of teaching and much confusion of approach just at the point where the child most needs a clear and definite course of instruction. In the past this instruction took the form of lessons in perspective and representational drawing in the nineteenth-century manner. Art teaching often tended to degenerate into copying or some form of derivative art. Present-day art teaching is often divorced from life. The adolescent is growing up in an exciting world of scientific achievement, of new patterns of living and of a rich variety of artistic expression. Today scientific creation and artistic invention are both expressions of the same vital energy. All too often the pupils with most intellectual and creative ability fail to develop any interest in art because they are not given a clear course of development that includes, for example, experience in handling materials, constructional work and experiments that correspond to the sort of work done in the school laboratory. Headmasters have been known to discourage an artistic career on the grounds that their best scholars were 'too good for art'. Yet it is becoming clear that we require more architects of a high calibre to cope with the vast new schemes of town planning and rebuilding which are, and are likely to be for some time, a feature of our civilization. Industrial designers are becoming key men in the commercial success of many products. They must be able to assess the artistic quality of a variety of materials, to argue the merits of their designs on boards of management and to appreciate the technical difficulties of production.

Most pupils do not wish to follow an artistic career, but it is the job of the teacher to make clear the relevance to everyday life of art as a subject. How many people know when shopping how to make an intelligent choice between different articles displayed? Consumers need a background of knowledge that derives from experience and education in order to be able to judge an article's fitness for their particular needs. Too often, goods, too expensive to replace, are selected and bought on the whim of the moment so that their owners come to dislike them. Art education will get the attention it deserves when students see that something of real value is offered.

This book aims at presenting a course of studies in creative work which will deal with various aspects of sensory experience. If rightly used it can provide plenty of opportunity for the development of aesthetic sensibility. But teachers in search of 'a method' can all too easily reduce any system to a series of gimmicks. It is important to realize that success in a Basic Course, or for that matter in any system of art teaching, depends on the contact between teacher and pupil. The teacher needs to give firm guidance but at the same time maximum freedom for the pupil to make his own discoveries. A sense of proportion and a knowledge of colour are essential to adult life. If these are based on personal discovery through careful analysis and experiment, the student will acquire confidence and develop a creative attitude to life and to his work.

The method of using the Basic Course will vary with the teacher and the needs of the particular class or individual child. There is danger in an over-dogmatic approach which is fatal to creative work. It has been found that the Basic Course is of special value during the early years in a secondary school in order to establish a foundation, but this does not mean it should necessarily be studied all the time. It must always be borne in mind that what matters most is the creative development of the child. What the Course does offer is a framework of experiment whereby the individual is given basic visual and tactile experience from which creative activity will flow. Children who are specially interested in figurative work will be all the more able to compose satisfying pictures if they have had the opportunity of experimenting freely with isolated aspects of visual experience, though the transfer of experience can never be taken for granted. It is the job of the teacher to coordinate and relate all the work done in the art department.

The needs of the class and of the individual must always be borne in mind. Thus the teacher may prefer to let some children, who have ideas to express, work at individual picture-making while the rest of the class are working on the Basic Course. Children learn from each other even if the work they are doing is different. The Basic Course can be varied by following time spent on, say, 'area division' in black and white, with a study of colour, or work in three dimensions.

The suggestions for further study and experiment at the end of each chapter should be regarded as possible lines of development which might be expected from students rather than as set exercises for the teacher to 'fall back on'. At the same time it must not be forgotten that good work will come only from clearly realized aims. The children should find out for themselves, and experience the joy of developing their art from the basic ideas.

It is important that the teacher should constantly vary his approach to the Basic Course. Fresh ideas are vital for creativity. The teacher must free himself, as well as the child, from outworn ideas about the conventions of art. The introduction of new media and materials, as well as suggestions from the students themselves, will all provide new avenues of experience.

It is also important that the Basic Course should come to have relevance for and to bear upon all types of work done in the art department. The Basic Course will be of little value if it is used merely as a marginal study; rather it should be used as a foundation for the whole course of art studies in the secondary school.

Chapter 1

The point

One of the first exercises in a Basic Course in art should be the examination of the 'point' as a means of covering space. By 'point' we mean an aesthetic entity that ranges from a regular shape, such as a small round or a small square, to an irregular amorphous shape. The exercises in this chapter are to help the student to find aesthetically satisfying arrangements of points in space.

It is important to establish the right approach from the start: (a) by arousing interest; (b) by stressing the need for personal discovery; and (c) by having clear aims and pursuing systematic methods.

Firstly, interest may be aroused by showing the relevance of the work to everyday life – the arrangements of flower-heads in a vase, a group of small pictures or drawings informally arranged on the art-room wall. Photographs of birds flying, or raindrops on a window-pane, could be examined. The arrangement of people in a crowd scene on a stage with different levels, or for a simple family photograph – particularly from the point of view of head positioning – and reproductions of Japanese prints or paintings, could be studied. A careful choice of examples must be made so that the point motif is the dominant structural element – it could be swamped by other factors.

Secondly, the pupil develops his creative ability only by personal discovery. The approach can be compared to that of scientific experiment. The difference is that the art student is discovering the principles of creative activity, not a dogmatic form of words or a formula. The task of the teacher is a difficult one, because he must stimulate and guide but he must never be dogmatic. He must not tell the student he is wrong, but let him find out for himself that he is wrong. The method is one of cultivated observation. Observation in this context is not limited to the visual, but must include feeling and touch.

Lastly, the need for clear aims and for a logical sequence of thought will not be easy to establish with the young adolescent in the secondary school. Art is confused with an ability 'to draw' or some mysterious process which defies analysis. The aim of this course is to give a basic training in form. Everyone has a natural sense of form. It shows itself first in the child's joy at discovering his toes and then the pleasures of simple shapes like a ball or a brick. The student needs to re-discover a love of simple forms. The beginner tends to hide his lack of knowledge and understanding by a display of over-elaboration. This may impress a superficial observer but the teacher must realize that this is a way whereby the student avoids the real problems and loses himself in meaningless decoration and complexity. Equally it is important to avoid a happy-go-lucky approach. What must be stressed is the need to let one idea follow another in an orderly sequence. The pupils should not be allowed to get bogged down with symmetrical or repetitive pattern arrangements. This is an easy way out. The aim is to use space positively rather than decoratively. To use space positively is to place each point with thoughtful care and understanding.

The first exercises could be carried out with thin sticks of charcoal and large sheets of cheap paper such as lining-paper or baker's wrapping-paper. Perhaps twelve or more drawings could be set out in an orderly but informal arrangement on the sheet, but the pupil should be discouraged from subdividing the paper with straight lines as this introduces a complicating factor which is best avoided at this stage. He could start with two points and their arrangement in space and then progressively move on to three and more.

As a change from working in charcoal, and to deal with more complicated arrangements, small black cut paper squares ($\frac{1}{2}$–1 in.) could be introduced. These allow an easy method of quickly trying different spacing before pasting down. The teacher will find it convenient to collect a box of paper squares. Offcuts of black and some grey papers can be trimmed with a guillotine to squares of different sizes. The square shape is used because this is more easily cut out than a round, but this new shape is now another factor with which to reckon. Some pupils will want to try turning the squares at angles to one another. The teacher needs a firm hand to ensure that too many new ideas do not lead to a lack of unity and confusion. The student is best helped if the problem is presented to him in precise terms. Success will invariably follow. One student could be encouraged to explore contrasts of size, another to introduce slight angles in the positions of the squares, another to modify the exact squareness with scissors so that each 'point' is different. Some may wish to explore overlapping or touching squares or to use another shape altogether. It does not matter in what direction ideas are leading or, indeed, if the work suggested here overlaps that of any other chapter, so long as the desire for creative experiment is retained and the student is making his own discoveries.

It is suggested that all early work should be in black and white. The mind is thereby set free to concentrate on one thing at a time. Limited colour can always be introduced when interest is seen to flag (see Chapter 9 on *Colour*).

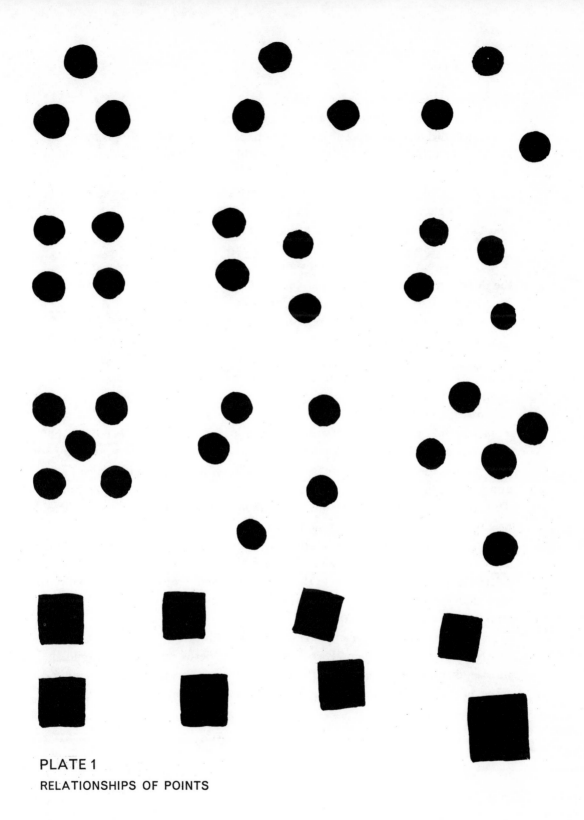

PLATE 1
RELATIONSHIPS OF POINTS

Suggestions for further study and experiment

1. Black and white points on a middle-grey ground.

2. Spots of black waterproof ink on wet paper, or spots of white poster-paint applied to a surface of black paint which is still wet. This provides an introduction to 'texture' or surface quality.

3. The use of small areas of white wax crayon defined with an all-over wash of freely applied, dark-toned watercolour. The new idea this exercise reveals is that one can see the point itself as a spatial entity, i.e. a hole.

4. Arrangements based on play with matches (see Chapter 8).

5. The display of butterflies in a showcase, the mounting of leaves on a card, the design of stars for the coloured ceiling of a room, or arrangements of balls for a frame on the principle of an abacus.

6. Point development, i.e. shapes other than the spot or square.

7. The relationship between points and straight or curved lines. If curved lines are used it could be suggested that each line should vary in width from thinness to thickness throughout its length in such a way as to strengthen the quality of the curve. The latter could be painted with a small pointed water-colour brush of good quality.

8. Large numbers of points freely placed on paper without any preconceived design. If desired, overlapping points could be used in certain places so that in these places the areas between the points take on a special significance. The aim here would be to develop the more intuitive or irrational side of the mind. The design could be worked out using shapes of similar size such as those produced by a flat brush or a poster pen.

9. Simple square shapes torn from white paper and arranged on a dark-grey ground. If there are straight edges on some of the pieces these should be considered as an additional factor in the design. In looking at the whole it will be seen that the areas between the shapes are bounded by some edges that are straight and some that are jagged.

In all these exercises it should be emphasized that two opposing factors are involved – the shapes themselves and the spaces between them. It would be unwise to think of the latter as a 'background' since this would suggest something of little or no importance. All spaces in the composition should have equal consideration.

PLATE 2

Students' experiments with points
including variation in size and tone.

(*top left*) Not touching. Girl age 12.
(*bottom right*) Touching. Girl age 12.
(*top right*) Point development. Boy age 12.
(*bottom left*) Intuitive design. Girl age 13.

Chapter 2

The development of the square

What is a good shape? That is a question not easily answered. We find a variety of shapes in nature but even those which seem to be complex have an underlying simplicity which gives the whole a unity and completeness that is satisfying and admirable. On the other hand, even a simple assemblage of mechanical parts is often lacking in proportion and balance.

The answer to the question depends very much on the purpose we have in mind. We might start by considering a perfect square. It has a quality of stability and completeness. It is related to a circle. While it remains strictly geometrical, apart from varying its size there is not much that one can do with it. But when we lengthen the sides to make a rectangle it has much more possibility of development and is, therefore, more interesting. A shape must contain diversity within its wholeness if it is to avoid boredom.

The teacher might begin by showing the class a large square of black paper against a white background, placing alongside it similar pieces equivalent to a square and a half, a double square, and a square and approximately a third, and then discussing which is the best shape. If we always used square paper for drawing on it would impose limitations for picture-making, whereas rectangular shapes occur in a wide variety of proportions and there is the added possibility of using the paper in the horizontal or vertical position to suit the type of subject. Some cameras give a square picture so that the instrument can always be held in the most convenient position, but the finished print is trimmed to a rectangular shape in the process of enlargement. When an architect is planning a building, it is possible with upright, rectangular windows to give dignity to the interior or exterior; on the other hand, rectangular windows in the opposite direction can suggest breadth and supply balancing horizontal lines. Square windows would not do this unless they were lined up to form horizontal bands as are seen in some skyscrapers. A rectangular table has certain advantages over a square table in the furnishing of a room because, for instance, it can be arranged with its long side against a wall to leave more space in the centre of the room.

Most books are rectangular in shape because not only are the proportions

THE SQUARE

The addition of the
half square gives
movement downwards.

Too obviously a double square?

Sloping sides: (*above*) 2 sides.
(*right*) 4 sides.

More subtle square shapes.

Stages in the development from a square to an asymmetrical curved shape.
Suitable for lino-cutting.

Examples of likely developments of the square.

PLATE 3

then more varied and individual, but also the book, especially if it is large, is easier to hold in the open position.

The teacher might go on to consider the advantages and disadvantages of shapes which are not strictly geometrical squares or rectangles, e.g. the windows of a motor-car, a 'contemporary' table with curved sides and rounded corners, a hand-made ash-tray in pottery-ware which is asymmetrically shaped. These new shapes are in harmony with an age of speed and change and serve to soften the harshness and geometrical form of many inevitably machine-made materials.

After discussion on these lines, practical work could consist of developments from the absolute square, using charcoal, or a brush and black paint. It is important that the shapes, when drawn, should be blacked in as soon as possible, so that the shape is considered rather than the line. The students should work freely on a fairly big scale so that the shape can be clearly appreciated and any unintentional irregularities will not then distress them. Some of the possible developments are as follows:

(a) 'Squares' with sides that are sloping or curved.

(b) Combinations of a 'square' shape with a line or a point, e.g. the line inside the square or partly inside.

(c) 'Squares' that have a piece 'cut out'.

While the class is working, the teacher should point out any accidental arrangements of 'squares' on the page which are interesting in their relationship to one another.

Suggestions for further study and experiment

1. Some of the accidental arrangements of 'squares' that have been found pleasing could be used as a basis for further compositions. Care should be taken to consider their placing in relationship to the edge of the paper. This is an exercise related to the work in the first chapter. It helps to develop a feeling for right balance or a sense of equilibrium in space. Finish in black and, if desired, grey on white paper.

2. Paste a 'square' of black paper on a sheet of grey, carefully considering its placing on the paper. Add one or more painted white lines and a small white square. The white square is to act as a focal climax. The focal climax or centre of interest is the centre or dominant part of the composition to which all other parts are related and which they enhance.

8

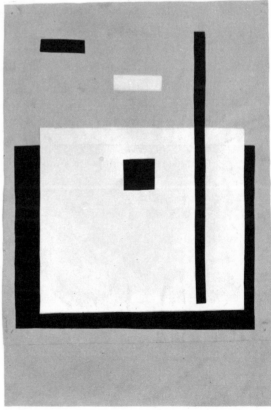

PLATE 4   (*top left and right*) Experiments with cut paper squares and overlapping
squares in ink and colour. Girl age 13.
(*bottom left*) Coloured wax crayon giving textural interest and tonal contrast. Age 12.
(*bottom right*) Development showing value of a centre of interest. Age 12.

3. Work out developments of a 'square' and a freely drawn circle exploring contrasts of size (there is already contrast in shape), different placings in the picture-space, and overlapping shapes.

4. Contrast two 'squares' in as many ways as possible – separately, over-lapping, or placed one inside the other.

5. Place a number of 'squares' one inside the other, making an asymmetrical design. Paint with a series of tones shading from black to white or with gradations of one colour. Notice the effect of recession.

6. Place a series of paper squares of equal size at close, even distances across the page like a mosaic, or a sheet of postage stamps. It should be noticed that if the squares are sufficiently close together one becomes more aware of the white lines, but if they are moved further apart the squares themselves become the dominant feature. Try to improve on this idea so that more interest is aroused, for example, by small variations of size or distance or by the introduction of slight angles.

7. Developments of the square can be tried out by means of lino-cutting. First make a print of a square of lino. Then make some modification of the original shape, e.g. by cutting one side at an angle. Make another print and continue in this way. The prints as they are made give the student a series of related ideas and introduce him to the idea of families of related forms. The method is somewhat equivalent to the process of carving, as the comparative difficulty of the material allows for a more contemplative approach.

8. Since it has four sides of equal length one can think of the diamond shape as a development of the square. (Notice, however, that it is more dynamic than the square.) Compose a design based on diamond shapes.

Chapter 3

Vertical and horizontal line arrangements

Two of our important psychological experiences are concerned with sensations of the vertical and horizontal. The vertical line suggests upward movement, and recalls the growing tree, the upright stance of man. It has a more vital quality than the horizontal, which is associated with calmness and repose. When vertical and horizontal lines of equal length are seen together, the vertical appears to look longer. Vertical lines tend to be especially noticeable in a landscape. These can be welcome when they are, for instance, in the form of a church spire providing a focal point and a contrast to the horizontal lines of a landscape. On the other hand objects such as lamp-standards and telegraph-poles all too often obtrude themselves in such a way as to give a feeling of unrest and discordance. A wooden 'post and rail' fence is generally more pleasing than one of concrete uprights threaded with horizontal wires.

Experiment will soon show that contrasts of vertical and horizontal, long and short, thick and thin, large spaces and small spaces, help to give variety and interest. Lines are to be seen not only as having value in themselves but as a means of creating spatial structure and rhythm. Repetition makes for a harmonizing rhythm provided it is not too geometrical. If it is too geometrical it becomes monotonous. Consider a row of trees or books on a shelf.

The points set out above, as with each chapter in this book, are hints for the teacher. They can be used as a method of starting off thought and discussion on the subject so that the student when he starts his practical work will have plenty of ideas to work on. It must be re-emphasized that composition and design cannot be taught intellectually by rules but only learned by searching and experiment – that is, by developing aesthetic judgement. Good design is founded not on science but on intuition and sensibility. It will be of great value if the student is constantly urged to look at nature (see Chapter 8). It is the constant interplay of discovery within and inspiration from without that will keep the imagination lively and prevent the exercises suggested in this and other chapters from losing their creative stimulus.

It is suggested that the class should be shown on the blackboard vertical lines which are an equal distance apart and of equal length and weight. A discussion

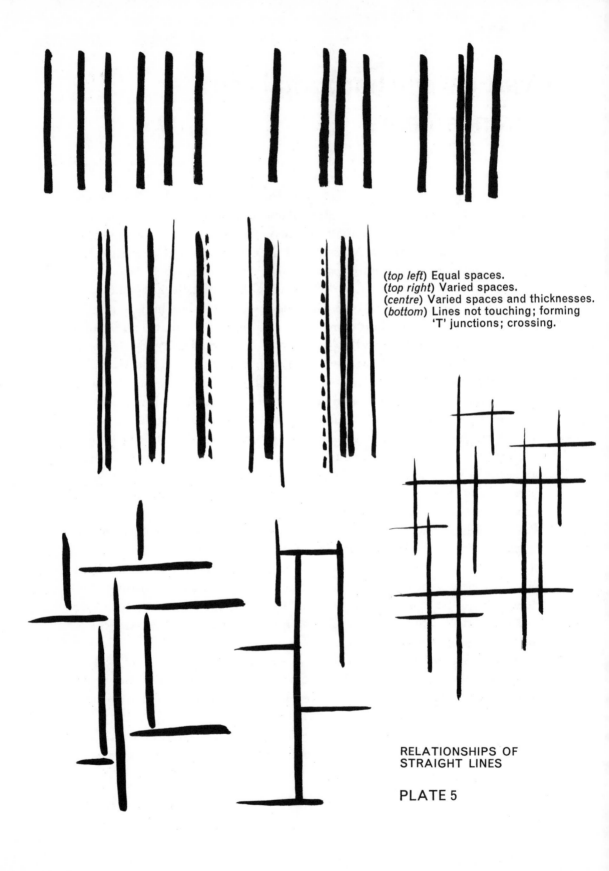

(*top left*) Equal spaces.
(*top right*) Varied spaces.
(*centre*) Varied spaces and thicknesses.
(*bottom*) Lines not touching; forming
       'T' junctions; crossing.

RELATIONSHIPS OF
STRAIGHT LINES

PLATE 5

PLATE 6 (*top*) Watercolour painted in vertical and horizontal lines with contrasting 'pools'
of colour. Boy age 12.
(*bottom*) Ink- and colour-work by girls age 13.
(*left*) Based on verticals and horizontals crossing each other. This has been given
added interest by the way in which the colour has been applied.
(*right*) Line arrangement of more subtlety using two pen widths. The whole forms an
asymmetrical shape.

will soon bring out ideas for improvement. Lengths can be varied, also thicknesses and distances apart. Dotted or double lines can be contrasted with single.

The practical work will consist of arrangements of either horizontal or vertical lines using a 'ball' script pen and waterproof black ink on cartridge paper. Some students find charcoal rather messy so it is as well to provide a change of medium whenever possible. A choice of pen widths should be provided. This exercise should be presented as a challenge to the student to produce interesting work within the severe limitations provided.

More varied arrangements can then be worked out using both vertical and horizontal lines. The teacher could at first insist on the drawings being done in one of three ways but not muddled together:

(*a*) with lines not touching each other;
(*b*) with lines touching and forming 'T' junctions;
(*c*) with lines crossing each other.

These can be worked out as before, i.e. as a series of exercises using a few lines at first and then, in succeeding exercises, adding more. It is useful to start with a main vertical or horizontal axis.

If desired, the work can be finished by using colour in such a way as to show up the lines (e.g. by leaving a white space between colour and line) and to add 'body' and contrast. The colour need not necessarily be used simply to fill the spaces between the lines. (This is the sort of work dealt with in Chapter 4 on *Area division*.) Use the solid quality of the colour to play a contrasting role to the linear quality and to strengthen the weak parts of the composition. Poster- or showcard-colour has more 'body' than watercolour and harmonizes better with dense black ink. If watercolour is employed it would be better to use a more transparent ink such as a blue or brown.

Suggestions for further study and experiment

1. More complex relationships of vertical and horizontal lines using two colours. Use ink, or poster-paint and a good brush, felt-tipped pens, or decorators' oil-paint squeezed straight out of the tube and drawn across the paper. The use of two colours, black (as dominant) and grey or light blue (as recessive) makes possible a design that can be conceived with an effect of depth.

2. Experiments with 'edge stencils' – that is, a stencil brush and nearly dry colour used against the straight-edge of a piece of thick paper to produce 'shaded lines' spaced across as desired.

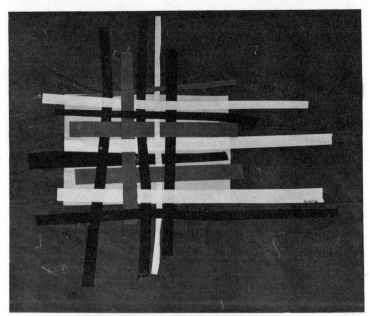
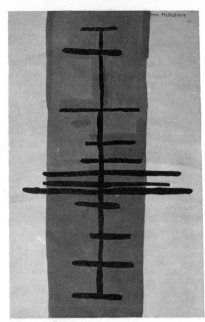

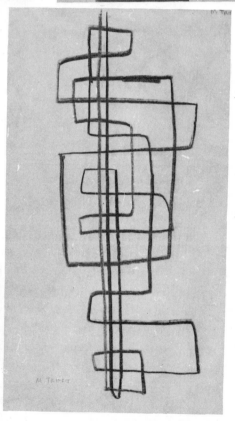

PLATE 7 (*top left*) Design based on paper cutting. A centre of interest has been created by some interweaving of the strips. Boy age 12.
(*top right*) Spacing of horizontal lines on a vertical axis. Girl age 12.
(*centre left and bottom right*) Typical charcoal drawings by girls age 13 exploring with a continuous line.
(*bottom left*) Vertical and horizontal lines not touching. Ink and colour. Boy age 12.

3. Line arrangements on grey paper using thin strips of black and white paper cut on a guillotine and then arranged and pasted down. A certain amount of interweaving of the strips can be tried.

4. Line arrangements in space using dowel-rod or wire (see Chapter 11).

5. Coloured wool or string wound round glass-headed pins stuck into a board. Coloured paper can be pasted under the lines if desired. The 'solid' colour of the paper provides a contrast with the thin lines of wool or string.

6. Line work combined with 'point' design.

7. Designs with a repetitive movement of equal-sized stripes. Here the aim would be to make the overall effect varied and lively in spite of using repetitive elements, by the use of varied tone and colour. This will serve to illustrate how tone and colour can alter apparent size.

8. Composition of a 'vertical theme'.

9. 'Taking a line for a walk' – this can be done in a number of different ways, some of which are described below:

(*a*) By standing in front of the paper and swinging a charcoal stick in a continuous line which freely explores the paper surface mostly in vertical and horizontal directions. It is best to practise this in the air above the paper until confidence is established. Work of this kind gives an opportunity to develop the intuitive side of the mind and certainly helps some students to free themselves from inhibitions. Success comes from relaxing the mind and drawing with a free arm rather than the cramped wrist movement associated with writing.

(*b*) By starting from any point and drawing a continuous line which covers the area in straight lines and comes back to the starting-point. It is desirable that the areas enclosed should have some relationship with one another – thus one student could experiment with rectangular enclosures, another with triangular shapes. Too many pointed angles are best avoided. Form is better when full in shape. When triangles are formed it is advisable to keep these of similar type, e.g. equiangular or right-angled, to ensure harmony.

(*c*) By drawing two lines (or more) in similar or different directions to each other but both starting from a point on one side of the paper and proceeding to the opposite side. There is no reason why one line should not go straight across the other, cutting it to make rectangular or triangular areas.

10. 'Taking a line for a walk' can be developed into a spiral-like formation by drawing a series of squares with a continuous line and gradually pushing the square shapes as they are being drawn to the left (or right).

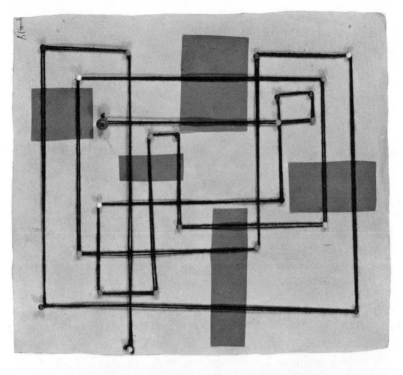

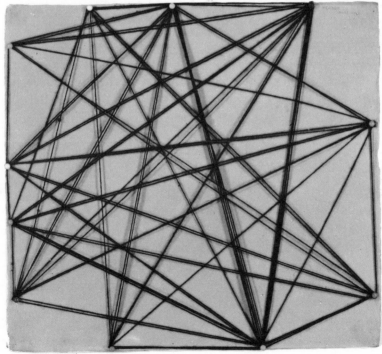

PLATE 8

(*top*) Lines in black wool using coloured glass-topped pins and cut paper. Boy age 12.
(*bottom*) In this case the line thickness has been varied by using different numbers of threads. Girl age 12.

Chapter 4

Area division

The painter when he begins a picture usually starts with a rectangular shape and this he proceeds to divide into orderly and related parts. Often these lines are parallel to the edge of the picture because this relates the pictorial composition within the frame. The horizon is often a horizontal line in the composition but it is extremely rare for this to come exactly in the middle. To place it there would tend to make the picture look divided and would, therefore, be less interesting, but the final effect depends, of course, on what is done with each half.

It should be noted that when a rectangle is divided equally by a horizontal line the upper division is apt to look larger than the bottom, giving a top-heavy effect. This can be demonstrated to a class by having a large square of black paper accurately positioned in the geometrical centre of a piece of white paper and comparing it with a similar piece placed at the optical centre. Other positions for the square could be shown, e.g. to the left or right of centre.

Certain theories have been held as to what constitutes good proportion. For example, artists have used a certain division of area known as the 'Golden Section' that establishes a particularly satisfying relationship between two parts. This can be defined in words as the division of a line so that the shorter length is to the greater as the greater is to the whole. It is approximately a proportion of 5 to 8.

Such knowledge is useful in an historical sense, particularly in analysing the work of many famous painters, but the 'Golden Section' is not the only basis of good proportion. What is most important is that, as far as possible, the student should discover good proportion for himself.

The teacher might also discuss with the class other traditional proportions, such as the area division of the pages of an open book, stressing the value of the margins in setting off the text, or the proportions of the panels and rails in a Georgian door. These should not be introduced in any dogmatic sense but rather to teach awareness and observation.

The practical work will consist in dividing up rectangles of different proportions into contrasting large, medium, and small shapes. A blackboard

1. Geometrical centre.
2. Optical centre.
3. More varied margins.

Proportions of a
book page.

PLATE 9   SIMPLE AREA DIVISION

demonstration could be made using straight-line division in one direction only, vertically or horizontally. Since the emphasis is on shape rather than line the areas can be painted in black and white. They can be alternated to give a 'counterchange' effect. These exercises in area division should also be used to teach tonal relationships. Thus a grey should be mixed which is exactly halfway between black and white. The method is to paint the proposed grey on a piece of scrap-paper which is held in turn against the black and against the white to see if there is a proper contrast with each. This grey can then be used along with the black and white to define the area divisions.

The class should proceed systematically with the practical work:

(a) using vertical and horizontal area division, drawing lines that are continuous from edge to edge of the rectangular space;

(b) using a mixture of continuous and short lines that are vertical and horizontal;

(c) using lines at slight angles to each other but avoiding triangular shapes. (Notice how sloping lines give a sense of movement.)

In each case the aim is to achieve the maximum contrast of large shapes against small, avoiding any two spaces being the same. There is a tendency at first for the student to produce far too many shapes without proper thought. It is most important to discourage this, and it can be avoided if the problems are tackled by using two, three, four lines and so on.

There is something to be said for working on a smaller scale in this particular series of exercises. Pencil is a change from large free drawing in charcoal and it helps to give confidence to some students. One should not be too dogmatic about the methods of drawing used, but ruler work is *not* to be encouraged as the ruler is apt to get in the way of a proper view of the paper which leads to mechanical or geometrical rather than visual, intuitional judgements. Assessment by eye is vital to satisfactory progress.

Suggestions for further study and experiment

1. Area division working on large sheets of printed newspaper. The newsprint can be turned upside down, the drawing being done with charcoal and the painting in black and white and (with permission) one other colour. Some areas should be left unpainted or should be painted only in a thin white as the print provides an interesting 'texture' (see Chapter 10).

2. Area division using 'L' shaped lines, or lines in the shape of a cross, or the like.

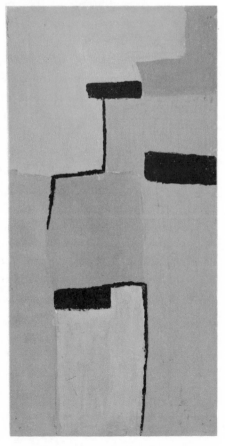

PLATE 10   (*top left*) A lively and rapidly executed piece of work based on 'taking a line for a walk'.
Other factors involved include: line thickness, contrasts of curved and straight lines,
areas of varied tone contrasted with quieter areas. Girl age 14.
(*top right*) The work of a boy who cannot draw in the conventional sense but who shows
a thoughtful approach to shape, tone and colour. Age 14.
(*bottom left*) Area division involving circles and squares. Girl age 13.
(*bottom right*) Composition in yellow with accents of black. Girl age 16.

3. Lino-cuts using vertical and horizontal division and worked out as a counterchange design (that is, of contrasting black and white shapes without lines). Once again the lino can be cut in stages and a print made after each cut. This method encourages the growth of ideas and an awareness of the relatedness of each act.

4. Area division using black and grey paper cut and arranged on white and then pasted into position. Painted lines could be added. Alternatively, small squares of coloured 'flint' paper could be provided. These should be chosen so as to make a good tonal contrast to the light or dark areas on which they are pasted.

5. A mosaic-like arrangement of rectangular shapes of different size using coloured paper pasted on to a grey background or alternatively shapes of scrap lino in various colours which can be stuck on to wood, the gaps being filled with 'Polyfilla'.

6. Area division to try out various colour exercises, e.g. a predominantly warm, or cool, colour scheme. The colours could be based on a study from nature.

7. Experiments with overlapping colour, using coloured tissue or coloured 'Cellophane' or watercolour. Rectangular shapes could be used or shapes based on a free interpretation of a letter of the alphabet.

8. Area division worked out from horizontal lines contrasted with lines at an angle to the vertical (say 80°). One or more circles could be added to re-establish the balance.

9. Lines at angles to each other producing triangular shapes of similar type to ensure harmony of form.

10. Designs using black and white shapes that read equally well as white on black or black on white. The shapes are best cut out in black paper and moved about on white until the best positions are found. They can be pasted on a grey background. It will be found that the designs read best when the areas of black and white are approximately equal and when the separated areas of black (and equally the white shapes) bear a relationship to each other.

Chapter 5

The development of the circle

The circle, like the square, is a basic shape with its own quality of completeness. It should be noticed that its aesthetic appeal and even its shape are influenced by varied spaces around it. Yet in its geometrical form its appeal is limited. For this reason, in naturalistic pictures its shape is frequently disguised, as, for example, when the moon is shown half-hidden behind a chimney-pot. But the basic shape can be developed in all kinds of ways to give rich possibilities.

The *ellipse* is a slightly more complex shape than the circle since it is made up of a number of different radii. The *egg-shape* is a particularly satisfying shape since it has a curve of very subtle variation and a difference of curvature at either end. Rounded pebbles may have even more variations of curvature and are in fact *natural sculpture*.

The teacher should have on display a variety of natural objects that are related to the circle: pebbles, shells that show spiral formation, rounded seed and fruit, bulbs and flowers. We take particular pleasure in these shapes because they have qualities of rhythm, harmony and good proportion. Rhythm comes into every work of art. It is fundamental to music and poetry as well as to the visual arts. Its quality can best be appreciated by studying natural objects that have been harmoniously fashioned according to the laws of growth.

A warning must be given here. We must not think of rhythm only as repetition or as something pertaining to easy curved lines. Students, however, should not be bothered about theories or detailed analysis, though it must be appreciated by the teacher that some children will find this section difficult at first. It is only with increasing confidence and mastery that their work will come to have a truly rhythmic quality.

As a first exercise, the class could fill in a large irregular shape with charcoal, working on cartridge-paper. Then they should work round this shape with a soft rubber, smoothing away irregularities until a sharp-edged form is obtained which is asymmetrical and has a wide variety of curves, varying in straightness in places as a result of this method of working. The process in fact is rather like that of making a spherical shape dealt with in Chapter 11 on *Three-dimensional art*. If desired, the charcoal shape could then be painted a dark-grey colour but especial care will have to be taken in painting the edge, which could be darker still.

Following this, the class could work out various developments of the circle, using charcoal and a large sheet of paper and setting out the exercises in a free but orderly way. Each shape should be filled in with charcoal as it is made and special attention should be paid to the edge. In fact, the edge could be slightly stressed with charcoal, as this helps to give the shape a feeling of unity and completeness. Once again the teacher should draw attention to any accidental arrangements of shapes in pleasing relationship to one other.

Some students could further explore the possibilities of segments of a circle or circles with parts cut away. It is important here that they should appreciate the difference between symmetrical and asymmetrical forms.

In general, asymmetrical forms will be more interesting than symmetrical because the latter are too obvious and static. However, a symmetrical form need not be despised provided it is deliberate. It is seen in a 'thrown' pottery shape because of the process by which it is made, and also in the design of a building that calls for formal grandeur. What must be avoided is a feeling of hesitation between symmetry and asymmetry, as this spells weakness and indecision. In the same way, there must not be competing themes, or two or more centres of interest, in a composition, or exactly equal areas of dark and light tone or a picture-space which is cut into equal areas. These are con-clusions which may well emerge when discussing the result of a class exercise.

Suggestions for further study and experiment

1. The circle in relationship to area division. Vertical and horizontal lines could be introduced to contrast with and divide the *inside* of the circle. Variations of one colour, or black, white and grey, could be used.

2. Or the procedure could be reversed – the circle being painted in a single tone or colour and some contrasting tones or colours being used *outside* it. The divisions need not necessarily be parallel to the edge of the paper. If radiating lines are used these lines might overlap the circular shape. It should be emphasized in all these exercises for further study that the student must avoid 'jazzing up' his design. Every line must be added with thought and care so that it contributes to the whole effect.

3. Circles inside each other. The student should endeavour to improve on the 'bull's-eye' target though this could be used as a starting-point.

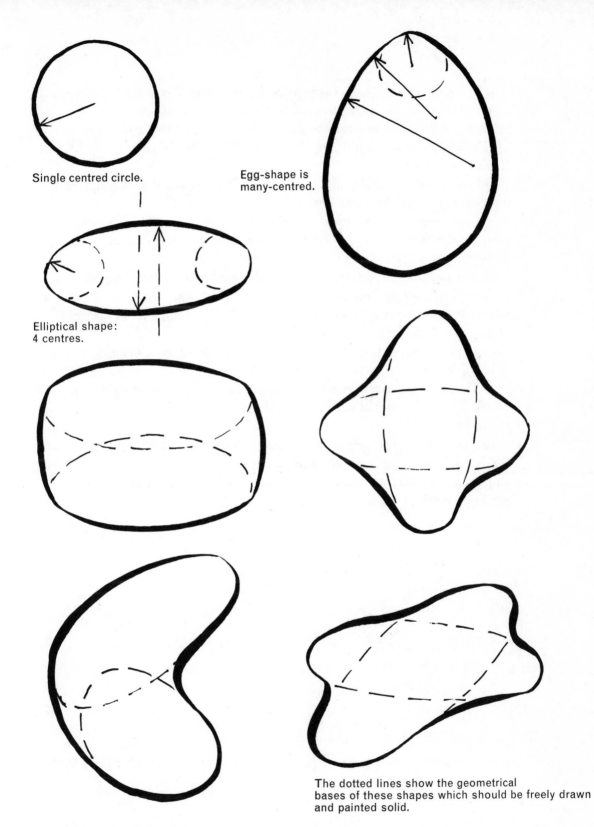

Single centred circle.

Egg-shape is
many-centred.

Elliptical shape:
4 centres.

The dotted lines show the geometrical
bases of these shapes which should be freely drawn
and painted solid.

PLATE 11   CIRCLE   DEVELOPMENT

4. Snowflakes (based on six points), stars (based on five or more points), or crystal forms, as the basis of creative designs but avoiding a mechanical geometrical basis. These could be painted in white on black paper.

5. A series of circles interlacing. These would be like the ripples from stones falling into a pond.

6. Circles of different size placed in a grid of rectangular shapes, and painted in primary colours plus black and white.

7. Developments of the circle and the spiral made by attaching a piece of paper to a pottery wheel and letting the wheel revolve slowly against different pressures and movements of a brush loaded with paint.

8. Straight lines of varying lengths, radiating from a common centre and making a regular or irregular circular shape. This idea could be developed further by means of a series of lines that cross the radiating lines in the manner of a spider's web.

9. Experiments with radiating lines, arranging and then glueing thin sticks of equal length, or matches, on to thin coloured card. This suggestion differs from the last in as much as the lines produced cannot start from a common centre (since the pieces of wood cannot be superimposed) and each line will be of the same length.

10. The circle developed as a point design. Using a brush and ink, a circular shape could be freely covered with points. The edge of the circle could be emphasized by making the points that are near the edge larger or closer together or overlapping.

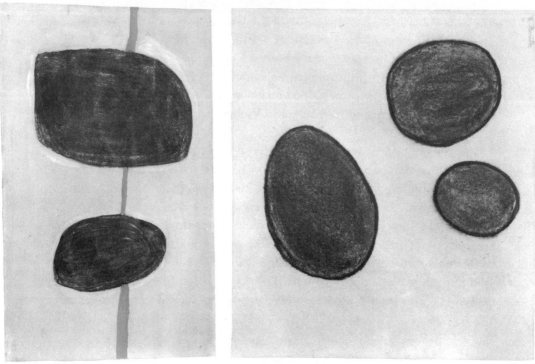

PLATE 12   *(top)* Contrasts of squares and circles, using black and a spotty-textured paper. Boy age 14.
(bottom left and right) Charcoal studies. Girls age 13.

Chapter 6

Curved lines

Before starting, the teacher should collect a variety of objects of good curvilinear shape such as leaves, trumpet- or bell-shaped flowers, pottery or silver-ware. From these, a series of analytical outline drawings should be made for the benefit of the class. The objects should then be placed on or beside the drawings so that the two can be compared. It takes a trained eye to see accurately the subtlety of curvilinear shapes and any help the teacher can give will serve to put the student on the right lines. The illustrations show some ways of analysing curves. In general, it should be remembered that it is the angle made with the vertical or horizontal that characterizes each curve. For this reason it is helpful for the teacher to see that vertical or horizontal lines appear in the background when drawing figures or when setting up still-life groups that contain round objects. Lines can be thought of as directions of force and the points at which they change or cross are of special importance.

Further help to a class could be given by showing drawings or photographs of, for example, the 'ogee' curve in fourteenth-century English architecture. The almost mathematical precision of the Greek vase might be compared with the less subtle form of the Roman, or reference might be made to the organic shapes of Chinese pottery. Curves have an emotional quality just as much as straight lines. Where the straight line stands for strength the curve conveys a quality of grace and sweetness. Too much 'curliness' in a design gives a flabby, weak effect. This can be seen in some Victorian pattern design and in badly drawn lettering.

The student will now be ready to draw lines for himself. He should begin by examining two curves in relationship with one another, but separated. This could be followed by two curves touching, crossing or growing one out of the other.

If possible, these exercises should be done by means of direct brush-work on large sheets of paper. Flabby inferior brushes are worse than useless. Sable watercolour brushes (about size no.6), which have springy points, could be used with thin black poster-colour. The colour should be thin so that it flows easily. The aim should be to produce strong rhythmic lines with the natural

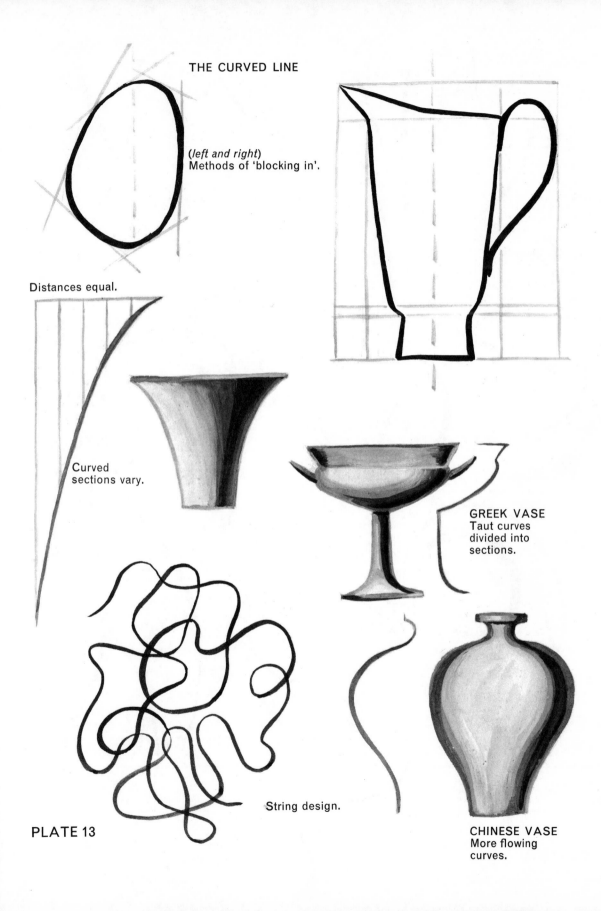

THE CURVED LINE

(left and right)
Methods of 'blocking in'.

Distances equal.

Curved
sections vary.

GREEK VASE
Taut curves
divided into
sections.

String design.

PLATE 13

CHINESE VASE
More flowing
curves.

RELATIONSHIPS OF CURVED LINES

PLATE 14

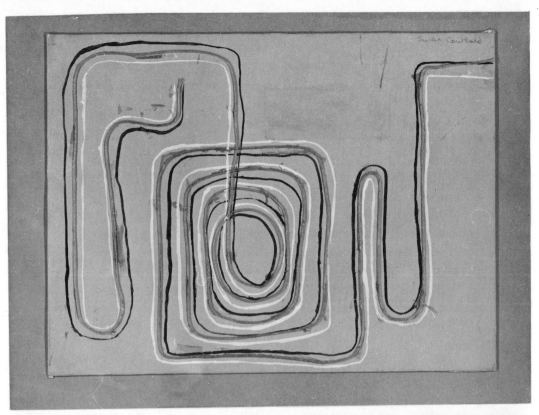

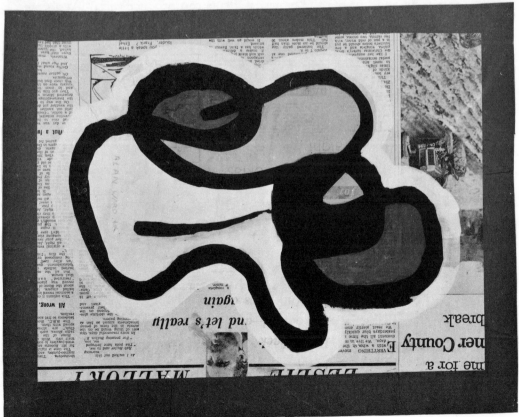

PLATE 15 (*top*) Linear design using string and paint. Girl age 13.
(*bottom*) Painting on newspaper. Boy age 12.

variation in thickness that comes from free arm movements with the brush. Free arm movements are also encouraged by using a steeply sloping drawing-board. Alternatively the student should stand to work at a horizontal desk, or kneel on the floor.

Suggestions for further study and experiment

1. *Free pattern in colour.* A series of curves, either overlapping, or touching, or separate, should be drawn across the paper from top edge to bottom edge. The spaces can be coloured using contrasts of light and dark, warm and cool colour (see Chapter 9 on *Colour*) and the lines painted in black.

2. *String designs.* These can be produced by dropping a piece of string on to a piece of paper until it forms a pleasing arrangement which can be plotted. Thick and thin string can be used together as well.

3. Straight lines and curved lines can be contrasted; either overlapping, or touching, or separate.

4. Students can prepare a series of scribbles and choose the best one for finishing.

5. Working in pairs, one holding the pencil on the paper and the other gently rocking and turning the paper, students can produce spiral-like forms.

6. Thick string can be glued on to card, or contrasts of thick and thin string can be used. This exercise could be completed by painting the whole composition with white paint thick enough to provide a unity of texture. Coloured string might suggest ideas for adding further colour.

Chapter 7

Curved shapes

The most useful illustration material for this section is a collection of water-worn pebbles, shells, and large bones. These three-dimensional forms can be studied by the class and translated into two-dimensional shapes, but it should be emphasized that the aim is not to produce carefully shaded naturalistic drawings.

Those students who find difficulty in drawing curved shapes may be helped by an analytical approach:
(*a*) by observing the extremities of greatest curvature;
(*b*) by 'blocking in' the rest using straight lines; and
(*c*) by adding the final outlines with delicate perception, and painting the shapes in black.

This drawing from natural forms will give confidence to students to invent their own shapes. If they already have confidence there is no need for this analysis. Analysis is only a means to an end and must not be used to an extent which spoils the spontaneous sensitivity of the student. It is the expressive quality of the line or shape that matters.

It should be noted that 'swelling out' shapes give fullness and charm provided they show a variety of curvature. Shapes that fall into two or more parts require special care, otherwise the connecting links look weak and unsatisfactory. A shape with a majority of almost straight-sided curves is stronger than one with too many 'flabby' curves.

The practical work in this section follows on that of the 'development of the circle' but now the students should concentrate on the relationship of two shapes. In arranging them together they will discover that the space left between becomes a factor of as great importance as the shapes themselves.

By superimposing one shape upon another a third shape is produced. This, too, has to be carefully considered in relation to the whole. A shape may be good on its own but unsatisfactory when used in this way with others.

When shapes are equal in size the result is uninteresting but when they are very unequal the result can be out of scale and discordant. All these things will be discovered by the student from practical experiment. Charcoal is the best

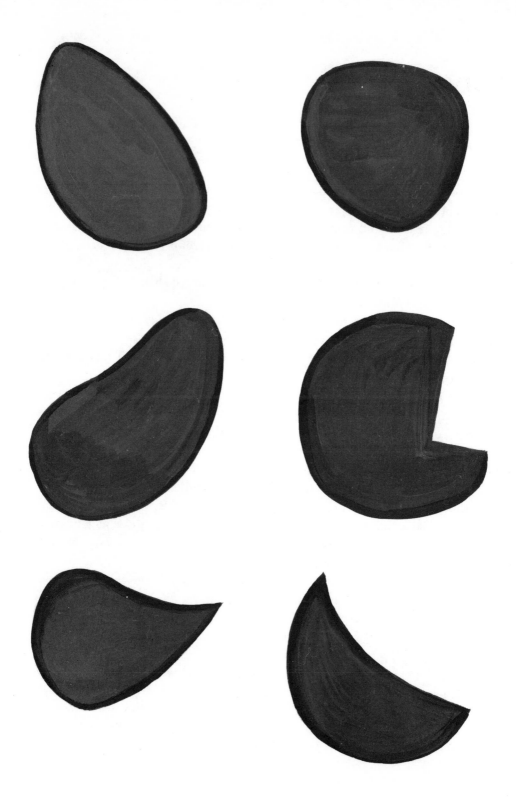

PLATE 16 SIMPLE CURVED SHAPES

PLATE 17   *(top)* Palette-knife painting using curved shapes. Girl age 16.
               (bottom) Curved shapes made by drawing contrasting lines from top to bottom.
               Painted in variations of one colour. Boy age 14.

medium and alterations can be carried out using a rubber supplemented by white poster-paint. In some cases the shapes can be cut out and pasted down in new positions after rearrangement.

Suggestions for further study and experiment

1. A relationship of three or more shapes.

2. Curvilinear shapes combined with lines – straight or curved. These can be worked out by arranging and pasting down cut paper shapes and then adding contrasting or linking lines. It is helpful to a class if themes are given such as 'flowing forms' or 'slim, pointed forms'.

3. Overlapping shapes worked out with coloured 'Cellophane' (or some similar coloured transparent material), so that a third colour is produced in the overlapping section.

4. A curvilinear shape contrasted with a straight-sided figure. A circular shape can be contrasted with a triangular shape or more complex shapes can be considered.

5. Curved shapes combined with area division involving straight lines.

6. One or more shapes, involving curved and straight edges, cut out in black paper and pasted on to white card in such a way as to create areas of white and black of equal value, i.e. so that the shapes will read as black on white and equally as white on black. This is excellent practice for reading with the eye in both a positive and negative way. Thus in drawing, say, a chair, the student can draw not only the structural features of legs and rails but also the areas in between these features. This is one of the ways in which the Basic Course can be linked with other aspects of art teaching, e.g. object drawing.

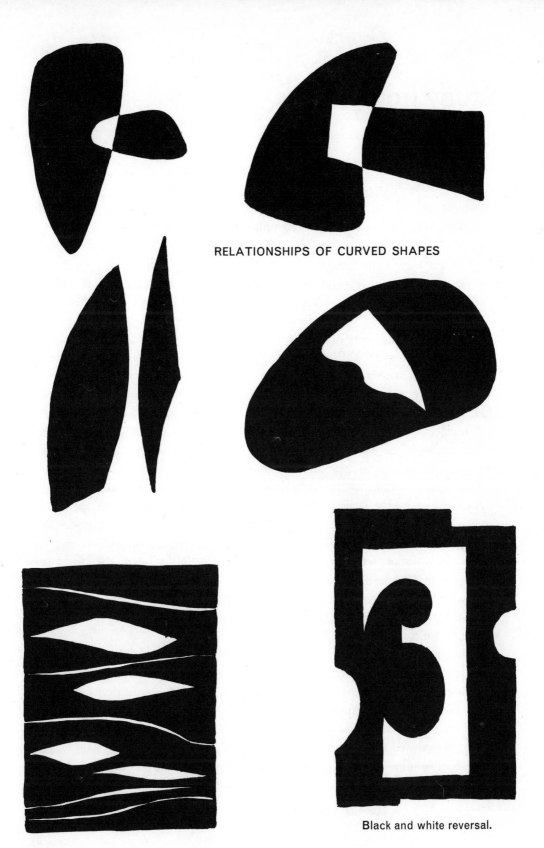

RELATIONSHIPS OF CURVED SHAPES

Black and white reversal.

PLATE 18

Chapter 8

Study from nature

Henry Moore has said that 'observation of nature is part of an artist's life, it enlarges his form knowledge, keeps him fresh and from working only by formula, and feeds imagination', but in order to observe properly it is necessary to avoid the mere superficial aspects of nature. That is why most benefit will come from nature study when some training in the Basic Course has already been undertaken. The approach must steer away from the decorative and naturalistic and seek rather the formal abstract qualities. Nor should studies be confined only to the more obvious forms of plant life such as trees and flowers. The study of basic art will help us to be more aware of the less obvious forms such as fungi, lichens, fruits, berries and vegetables, sections seen under a microscope, crystals, shells, stones, a piece of coal, the graining of wood, the bark of a tree, the cracking of dried mud or flaking paint, and also the natural and accidental arrangement of everyday things – pins spilled on a table, the coiling of cane, or railway-carriage windows seen looking through two or more trains that have stopped alongside one another.

All drawing should be selective in its approach and this is especially important in connexion with the Basic Course. What is needed is an analytical approach. At the moment we are not interested in naturalistic representation. The student needs to interest himself in some particular aspect which can be studied in isolation from the subject as a whole. Thus he might study the arrangement of radiating markings on a shell without drawing the shell itself, or he might consider the arrangement of seed heads on a plant without drawing the plant itself, or he might study the rhythmical line-pattern of coal structure without wishing to draw the broken lump of coal itself.

Students should bring an assortment of objects of good structural form that interest them. Some things will be provided by the teacher. To the list of suggestions mentioned earlier one might add: driftwood, stones that have been worn and polished by the sea, berries and nuts, sections of fruit such as an apple, or of a vegetable such as a cabbage, a sawn section of a log of wood, or a piece of polished wood with well-marked graining. Magnifying glasses will be needed as in many cases the drawings should be done on an enlarged scale to discover new arrangements of form. For this reason it is suggested that the cooperation of the science department should be sought. Microscopes and mounted slides will be useful, and it might be possible to borrow skulls or interesting crystals. There is much value to be gained from linking art with other subjects in this way.

Experiments could be carried out involving direct printing from nature, using leaves, slender stems, tendrils and rootlets. The method is to ink the plant material with a roller drawn in one direction only and to print it on to absorbent paper by rubbing, as is done for lino-cuts. This approach is useful for students who find difficulty in drawing and serves to suggest new aspects of line and form that are not always apparent just from looking at a plant.

Some aspects of nature that involve rapid movement can only be studied by means of photography, for example: big electrical discharges, or falling water. An easy way of recording arrested movement is as follows: a bunch of about a dozen matches is allowed to fall repeatedly on to a piece of paper until a satisfactory arrangement is seen which can be studied, either (*a*) by drawing the match *heads*, or (*b*) by drawing the *stems*. The drawing can be accomplished by plotting with a pencil direct on to the piece of paper and finishing with black ink or paint. A similar experiment could be carried out using a piece of string or two pieces differing in thickness.

Suggestions for further study and experiment

1. Creative arrangements of dried plant and other material could be set out between two sheets of glass or 'Perspex'. A spacing strip of card could then be inserted at the edge and the whole bound with tape.

2. A study could be made of a selected portion of plant life while it is still in position in (say) the hedgerow, to observe the rich variety of form and contrast.

3. A study could be made of all that is seen when a tuft of weed and grass is pulled up, or a stone turned over.

4. A study of the rhythm of growth could be undertaken. Thus a twig can be analysed in two ways, by measuring the intervals between the branching-points and also the total length of each twiglet, i.e. the distance from the tip of the leaf to the branching-point. These intervals can be plotted to form a grid which might provide, for example, a basis for area division. Similar analytical modes of study could be worked out for other things such as the spirals of a shell, or the student's hand.

5. *Colour analysis from nature.* A single flower or leaf could be taken and a careful record made of as many colours as can be found, not forgetting the shadow colours on the parts of the leaf or flower turned away from the light. Using a palette-knife, these colours should be freely placed near to each other and some regard paid to proportion so that the relative amounts of colour on the paper correspond to the relative amounts of colour found in the leaf or flower.

6. Summer and autumn give special opportunities for the study of colour, as suggested above. Winter reveals the bony, structural elements of nature. Leaf skeletons show branching and radiating relationships, and the dried dead stalks from summer plants show relationships of curved and straight lines. Ice which has been broken and re-frozen gives a pattern of irregular, superimposed forms. Springtime gives an opportunity to study the abstract qualities of budding forms or of melting snow.

7. The student can often be led to study more closely the way in which nature works by being presented with the problem of making a 'natural form' for himself. Chapter 11 on three-dimensional work shows how plaster can be shaped like the rounded forms found on the sea-shore. Thin card and wire can be cut and twisted to exhibit something of the rhythm and composition of growth forms. A start might be made with a single imaginary flower or a composition of three leaf shapes. Since cardboard has its own structural characteristics the approach should be abstract rather than naturalistic.

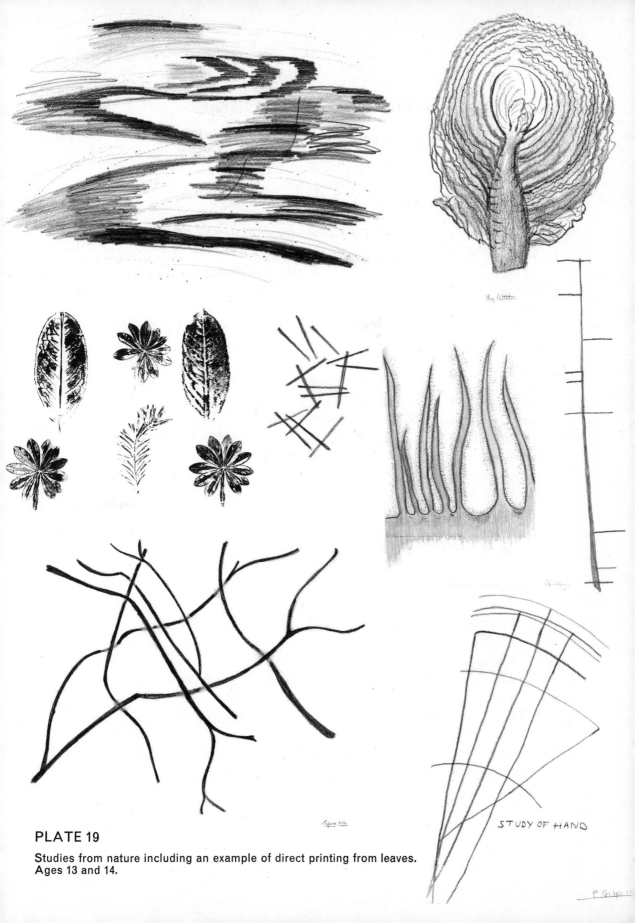

PLATE 19

Studies from nature including an example of direct printing from leaves.
Ages 13 and 14.

STUDY OF HAND

Chapter 9

The study of colour as basic visual experience

Colour theories as such are best avoided in the secondary school. We do not expect to be able to order colour mathematically, but everyone has some colour sensibility since colour is a basic visual experience. The young child usually has a very fresh and lively sense of colour, but his colour sensibility is often lost to fads and fashions – by the failure of the teacher to give any real training and opportunity for development.

Colour itself has no form but nevertheless it is the complement of form. It is less important than form, which is one reason why most of the preliminary exercises in the Basic Course should be in black and white. Yet bad colour can spoil good shapes and make a satisfactory composition into a meaningless jumble. On the other hand good colour can show up and highlight good shapes and convey qualities of mood and emotion.

The student has to learn how to mix colour and to relate one colour with another to produce harmony and contrast. Even the born colourist must have his colour sense strengthened by training. One aim of the Basic Course is to make the student's colour sense as precise as possible – which is not the same as making it neat and tidy. That is:

(a) He should be able to analyse a given colour sufficiently well to be able to match it by mixing pigment.

(b) He should be able to assess a colour accurately in terms of its tonal value and its warmth or coolness.

(c) He should be able to find a contrast to a given colour which provides a satisfying relationship. Once the student begins to get away from theory and develop his own visual judgements, he will be able to widen and develop his colour sense to an unlimited extent.

When we look at colour we can see that it has three properties: (a) Intensity; (b) Temperature; (c) Tone.

Intensity (or hue) refers to its brightness – its sensation of blueness or redness.

Temperature refers to its warmth or coolness. A blue may be quite centrally balanced but more usually it inclines towards greenness and coolness or towards redness and warmth.

Tone refers to the lightness or darkness of a colour; but it must be remembered that the tone of a colour can be changed by placing beside it a contrasting tone. In the same way the temperature and intensity of a colour will change according to the contrasting colour next to it. The quality of daylight or artificial light also affects colour and often makes nonsense of colour theory. We can only judge colour in terms of visual experience.

Now follow some practical recommendations:

(a) Poster- or tempera-colour are the best paints for basic art experiments in school. Oil-paint is expensive. Watercolour lacks 'body' so that alterations cannot easily be made. Nor does it easily allow colour to be used at its full intensity, and one colour cannot be placed on another.

(b) There is no advantage in the student having a large range of colours to start with. It is far better to have a few colours that he can get to know well and have confidence in using. The School Packs made by John Keep & Sons Ltd (15 Theobalds Road, London WC1) have been found particularly useful since they meet the problem of distribution and storage. Each pack consists of six basic colours and black and white. The 2-oz jars can be refilled from 5-lb tins.

(c) Flat palettes should be provided for mixing colour. These can be made from pieces of hardboard (say 10 in. × 7 in.) painted white. The flat board discourages the use of weak and watery colour and encourages the mixing of a large variety of colours. When there are wells in a palette the student tends to mix only one colour per well and too much of it.

(d) Palette-knives are particularly useful for colour experiments since the knife can be quickly washed and wiped on a rag with the certainty that it is quite clean. Also it is possible to see the colour on the knife and use it for matching purposes. The palette-knife helps the pupil to be aware of colour as a physical thing and to use it with full richness and intensity. A cheap substitute for the steel knife which is very satisfactory for school use usually goes under the name of a 'plastic paste-spreader'. Many students prefer these to the steel knives.

(e) Colour experiments should not be set out geometrically. No preliminary ruling of lines is necessary as this will make the lesson too formal and kill interest. Let the students spread fairly large squares of colour on to paper so that the value of the colour can be appreciated clearly and the colour is enjoyed for its own sake. If two colours are to be contrasted or related in any way let them be painted right next to one another so that the full effect

43

of the juxtaposition is seen. There is no danger that the colours will spread into each other if they are mixed to a proper consistency. Sometimes one colour can be placed on top of another, especially if the colour underneath is lightly scraped with a palette-knife. It is most important that as experiments proceed the names of the colours used should be written against each result, otherwise the student will forget how some of the colours have been mixed.

The class might first be divided into four sections, each section to examine one of the four principal colours available – red, yellow, blue and green. Does the blue, for example, tend towards warmth or coolness? What colour must be added to place it centrally – neither warm nor cool? What is the effect of adding white? With some dark colours the addition of a small quantity of white can create an increase in intensity. Having mixed a neutral blue of maximum intensity this should be painted in a fairly large square in the centre of the paper. A pale blue (obtained by adding white) can be painted on one side of it, on the opposite side a dark blue (obtained by adding black) and on the remaining two sides a warm blue and a cool blue. The remainder of the page can be taken up by using 'broken colour', that is, by the addition of small quantities of the opposite colour to blue, and also of black and white, to give a succession of blue-greys shading down to neutral grey. The aim is to examine blue in all its aspects while the rest of the class is similarly dealing with yellow, green and red. In the case of the last two colours the tone values should be adjusted so that the colour is neither light nor dark. It should be noted that when white is added to blue the result is still blue, but when white is added to red the result is a psychological change – pink. When black is added to yellow both tone and temperature change and it will be necessary to add, say, 'hazel brown' to make the yellow neutral.

Having examined the four principal colours the student might next mix the intermediate colours, but first he should set out in the middle of his paper a large patch of yellow, with blue near one edge and red near the other. Each colour should be at its maximum intensity and centrally balanced – neither warm nor cool. He will find that of these colours yellow is the lightest in tone value and blue the darkest. Then he should mix the intermediate colours, green exactly halfway in tone value between blue and yellow, orange exactly halfway between yellow and red, and finally the blue-green/yellow-green and the yellow-orange/red-orange colours to get the tonal value carefully graduated from one colour to the next.

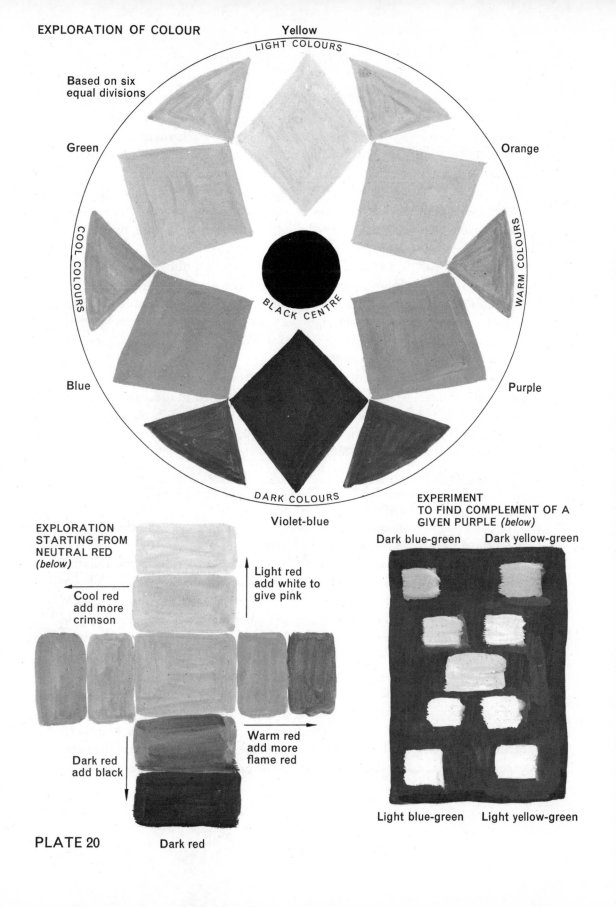

EXPLORATION OF COLOUR

Yellow

LIGHT COLOURS

Based on six
equal divisions

Green

Orange

COOL COLOURS

WARM COLOURS

BLACK CENTRE

Blue

Purple

DARK COLOURS

Violet-blue

EXPLORATION
STARTING FROM
NEUTRAL RED
(below)

Cool red
add more
crimson

Light red
add white to
give pink

Warm red
add more
flame red

Dark red
add black

PLATE 20

Dark red

EXPERIMENT
TO FIND COMPLEMENT OF A
GIVEN PURPLE *(below)*

Dark blue-green   Dark yellow-green

Light blue-green   Light yellow-green

Further experiments could be made with complementary colours, to find by visual judgement and experience the right complement to a given colour. For example, a large area of purple could be painted as a background and allowed to dry. Then a series of small patches of colour could be placed on this background with a palette-knife, ranging from light yellow-green to dark yellow-green and light blue-green to dark blue-green so that by inspection the right colour could be decided upon. Students should also have practice in analysing a given colour (which might take the form of mixing a pigment to match a given piece of coloured paper).

The teacher will devise other experiments according to the needs of the class. He will certainly need to explore the range of discord colours for himself but it is doubtful if the student under 16 should be encouraged to study this aspect of colour. The systematic study of discord is too confusing for the adolescent, but he should certainly be made aware of colour combinations in everyday life that are particularly pleasing.

Paintings can be examined for examples of discord. It will be noticed that in medieval painting, where the spots of discord are small in area, the clash is a bold one, whereas in modern painting, where there may be large areas of discord, the clash of colours is less drastic. Pink and orange, for instance, are less discordant than pale lilac and orange.

Suggestions for further study and experiment

1. Colours freely spread over the surface of the paper in an intuitive manner but aiming to achieve tonal and temperature contrasts.

2. With the help of the colour analysis suggested earlier, using the range of say, greens, for a landscape or woodland picture or for area division. The chosen colour theme, plus neutrals, to be used as far as possible before any other colour.

3. An analysis of colours from nature, e.g. in a marrow. The student should carefully match the colours and he could use these to produce a composition that uses the same colours in the same proportions (and possibly the same pattern) without copying the actual form of the marrow.

4. Experiments in mixing grey using complementary colours, e.g. yellow and violet-blue. These involve painting an area of, say, yellow and then further patches of yellow with increasing quantities of violet-blue and decreasing quantities of yellow until the unmixed violet-blue is reached. This exercise helps to show the wide range of colours that can be produced from two colours.

5. A colour circle, using six equal divisons. By making the design star-shaped, spaces are left between the points of the star for the intermediate colours. Starting with neutral yellow at the top, the colours should be carefully adjusted to get an even range of tone from the yellow which is light to the violet-blue which is dark. Thus the top half of the colour circle is light and the bottom half dark. One side is warm and the other cool. This exercise can be finished if desired by inking in the sections with a broad ball-pointed script pen and Indian ink and adding further lines to give an effect similar to a stained-glass window. The effect of the black is to make the lighter colours seem brighter by contrast.

6. A colour circle composed of 'shades', which can be painted in the middle, surrounded on the outside by 'tints'. A 'shade' is a colour with black in it; a 'tint' is a colour with white in it.

7. An analysis of the colours of a modern painting. The same colours can then be used in the same proportions in a non-representational design.

8. In the same way the colours of a shell or a flowering plant can be used in a design in the same proportions as found in nature.

9. A painted grid made up of squares of equal size. Here the aim is to make a rather monotonous design lively and interesting solely by contrasts of colour. Thus several squares can be painted with the same or similar colours and strong contrasts can be introduced where desired. The tone value of the colours used will be an important factor in the success of this painting. This exercise also gives a good opportunity for studying the spatial nature of colour – i.e. the effect of nearness or distance.

10. A 'juxtaposition' chart will show how the tone, intensity and temperature of a colour change according to the colour of the background. A strip of middle-grey stuck on a white background will look darker than a similar strip stuck on black. By masking the background the two strips of grey which look different can once more be made to look the same. Having tried grey, the same experiment can be carried out using other colours, e.g. yellow on black and white, and then violet-blue.

The class could afterwards be given a 'visibility test' to find the best coloured background to show up a given colour, e.g. vermilion-red could be tried against neutral colours, and then against different kinds of green, brown, blue, etc.

Chapter 10

Experiment with textures

All children are very much aware of surface qualities and materials when they are at the seaside – in the stones, the water, and the sand. Those brought up in the country are aware of the texture of dry-stone walls or ploughed fields. The process of weathering and ageing in natural materials takes on a richness and feel which give pleasure. The synthetic products of today are by their nature unsympathetic and require careful design if they are to give pleasure. Now that smooth machine-finish has become all too common we have come to appreciate all the more the work of the hand craftsman. It is still true that insensitivity to surface qualities tends to be a defect of those who live in cities and this is an aspect of art education that should not be neglected.

In introducing the subject of textures a collection of materials of interesting texture could be arranged in the art room. This should include man-made materials such as satin, velvet, netting and glass, and natural materials such as tree bark, smooth pebbles, fur and feathers. Some of these materials could be made up into two-dimensional designs. For example, fabrics, sandpaper, corrugated cardboard, newsprint, milk-bottle tops, could be glued on to cardboard. Paint could be added if desired. Alternatively, a piece of wood could be prepared, say 12 in. × 7 in., with an edging of strip wood $\frac{1}{2}$ in. × $\frac{1}{2}$ in., and inside this could be nailed some small-mesh wire-netting or expanded metal. Over this could be poured plaster of Paris (containing a little glue so that it will set slowly) or 'Polyfilla'. When the mixture is nearly set, a design can be created by inserting such things as the following: broken crockery, poultry-grit, pebbles, shells, netting, twigs and glass.

A more simple class exercise would be to create a design using two materials of the same colour but of a different texture, e.g. smooth white card and bookbinder's muslin.

The transition from the texture of actual things to that of drawn and painted surfaces can be bridged by making 'rubbings' on to thin paper with large sticks of black or blue wax crayon. Rubbings can be made of objects inside or outside the art room such as bricks, metal grating, cane-work, a kitchen-grater and ribbed glass. A series of prints one on top of the other can be made on absorbent

An arrangement of actual materials set in plaster.

Simple contrast of plain and
textured papers with added brushwork.

Suggested method of
mounting and linking
up textured material.

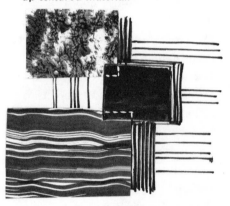

Pattern   Plain

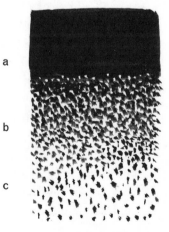

a

b

c

Stipple

Rough   Smooth   Another method of
contrasting textured
material.

PLATE 21

paper from pieces of corrugated cardboard that have been separately inked with different colours using rollers and lino-colours. By printing the corrugations at different angles to each other some interesting textured patterns can easily be obtained. These activities will find a ready response in any class, and students could be divided into two sections, a change being made at half-time. In a succeeding lesson textured papers could be used with plain black and white papers to form designs. A curved cut-out shape of an interesting texture could be contrasted with, say, a black straight-sided shape. After pasting these on to a suitable background further lines or colours could be added.

It should be made clear at this point that texture is not confined to repetitive pattern or to easy decorative effects. The teacher must bear in mind the more creative aspect and not present the subject in too mechanical or technical a manner. Reference could be made to the surface qualities found in everyday life such as those created by flaking paint, oil floating on water, and cloud formation, and to the fact that certain accidental formations can stimulate the imagination to give pleasurable or terrifying images. The experiments that follow give an opportunity to explore images of indeterminate shape and imprecise colour and to open up the intuitive world of sensations.

Paint or ink, or both, could be 'smudged' between pieces of paper, by folding or otherwise. If folded paper is used the image will be symmetrical but one half can be discarded if desired. The image created should be examined carefully and developed either by more smudging or by freely working on it with pen and ink lines, coloured pastel, or other media. Ink-smudging is best done using white paper but paint-smudging could be started using white paint on black paper and subsequently other colours could be added.

It should be emphasized that for all these experiments a wide variety of textured papers and of media should be provided since the aim is to develop senses of touch, feeling and intuition. In this way students will make discoveries for themselves. The palette-knife is itself a rich source of experience since the colour can be applied in a solid slab-like way that 'builds up' the idea. Thus the class could experiment with complementary colours of, say, red and green together with black and white, using the palette-knife and building up the idea of 'conflict'. Or a quieter composition could be made from two colours in close harmony. The subtlety of 'half-dry brushwork' could be explored using black and grey paint with cheap $1\frac{1}{2}$ in. or 2 in. flat brushes on lining-paper. This could then be worked over with pen and ink lines which would give a contrasting note of precision to the brushwork.

PLATE 22　Plain and marbled paper on grey paper with painted white lines.
(*top*) Girl age 14.　(*bottom*) Boy age 14.

Some experiments could be carried out with ink. For example, spots of waterproof ink could be allowed to spread in an accidental and irregular way on to wet cartridge paper. Alternatively, blobs of ink could be vigorously blown into star clusters or fern-like shapes or, with the paper and drawing-board tilted in different directions, persuaded to trickle into spirals or other patterns. These experiments are kept under better control if the teacher distributes the ink as required, as the students then have more time to study the effects already obtained (and incidentally to recover their breath) and generally put more thought into what they are doing. Black or blue ink is a good starting colour. A second colour is used only when no more can be done with the first colour. The work can be finished with the pen or with another medium such as watercolour. Experiments should be organized in 'making marks' using different kinds of pencils, crayon and brush. Our creative ideas are very much bound up with materials. This is most obvious with sculpture, but it is equally important in drawing and painting. Each kind of brush, pencil, pen or chalk makes a range of marks of a special kind and the student should be encouraged to explore these. The class could be divided into sections, each using a different medium, and results compared. Thus students could use black drawing-crayon in as many ways as possible – drawing with the side, the corner, smudging, rubbing, dotting and obtaining lines that vary in thickness, darkness, sharpness and straightness. If some individuals are uncertain what to draw they could be encouraged to record their feelings about subjects such as a whirlpool or an explosion, or to 'take a line for a walk' as though exploring the streets and squares of an imaginary town. This should serve to help the student to see the possibilities in drawing.

This type of experiment with technique should lead on to the creation of 'intuitive images' using black paint and brushes of varied sizes, including large house-painting brushes up to at least 2 in. in size. The attitude of mind is an important factor here, and the teacher must judge the right moment for introducing this type of work. Good results can only be secured by quiet, confident, and usually rapid manipulation of the brush, working in a purely intuitive manner, each movement following instinctively and reacting creatively to what has just been done before. Plenty of cheap paper should be provided so that a large variety of images, shapes and movements can be created. Then at leisure (and when dry) these can be studied from different angles. Anything not satisfactory can be discarded.

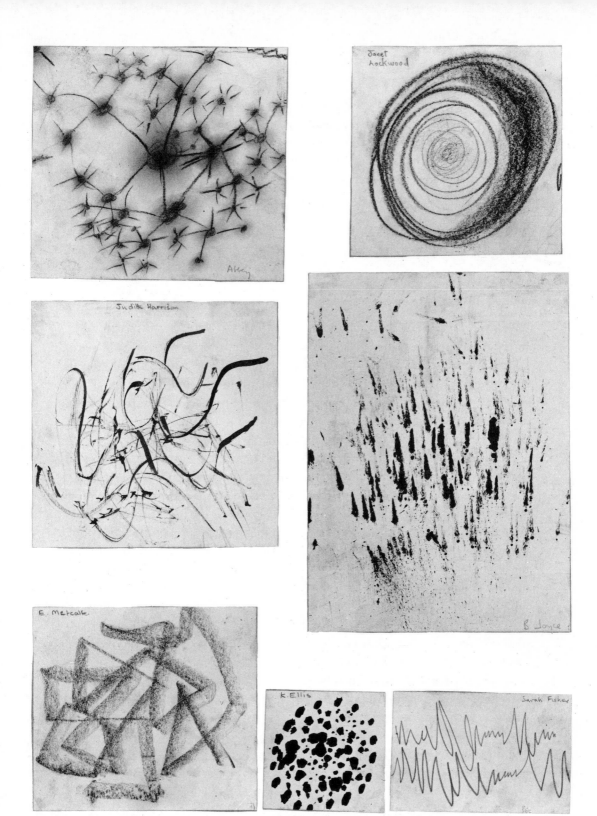

PLATE 23 Examples of 'making marks' with a variety of drawing media. Age 12.

Of course, some students are inhibited in their work and are frightened of being wrong. Even to make irrational aimless marks becomes difficult without the intervention of conscious thought. Results will come only when such students are encouraged to explore the unknown and, if necessary, to try deliberately for illogical placings and discordant shapes. Having worked through this phase, the student will be free to work both with the conscious and with the intuitive side of his mind.

Students often lose confidence in their work because art is equated with knowledge and cleverness, whereas of course the truth is that art is an activity natural to man.

Suggestions for further study and experiment

In all these exercises a most important part of the training in aesthetic sensibility lies in examining carefully the often accidental effects that are produced, and selecting those portions which have significance and meaning. These should be mounted on a suitable contrasting paper or a selected portion should be cut out and used with other cut pieces to form a design. It must be remembered that, in the words of Sir Herbert Read, 'Art is *ordered* expression'.

1. Wax resist – this technique involves rubbing a candle or white wax crayon over white drawing paper and revealing the tracings so made with watercolour.

2. Colour can be 'flicked', 'dribbled' or 'sprayed'. This is probably best done on the floor using large sheets of lining-paper with large 2 in.–3 in. brushes and large pots of paint in, say, three colours. Suitable protective clothing is essential. Flicking can be employed on a smaller scale by drawing a match-stick across the bristles of an old tooth-brush which has been charged with colour. Spraying can be done with a 'spray diffuser' – the sort used with charcoal fixative. Spraying can be used in conjunction with some sort of masking, e.g. a piece of old coarse netting, a shell or a cut-out shape. For dribbling it is best to use a plastic squeeze-bottle with a nozzle. White paint can be used on paper which has been painted black and which is still damp.

3. Various colours can be blended with cold water paste and spread quickly over smooth paper with a large brush or sponge. This can be drawn on, while still wet, with a cardboard comb.

4. Marbled effects can be obtained by floating diluted oil-colour on water and inserting paper underneath it, so that the textured design is caught as the paper is lifted up.

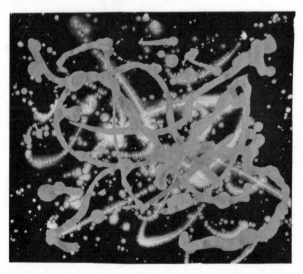

PLATE 24   (*top left*) Contrast of plain and paste-combed paper with added lines. Boy age 13.
(*top right*) Two examples of ink-blowing. Age 14.
(*bottom left*) Horizontal design on vertical axis using marbled paper.
(*bottom right*) Example of flicking and dribbling. Girl age 13.

5. Various lace-like materials in the same colour can be glued on paper of a different colour. Suitable materials would include scraps of lace, curtain net, embroidery canvas, scrim and paper doyleys.

6. Squares of textured paper in different sizes can be mounted on drawing paper so that they are overlapping or corner to corner and straight with the edge of the paper. A contrasting linking colour, either solid or in lines, can be used to join up and create a unity.

7. Small compositions on post-cards can be made using paper fasteners, clips, beads, etc. Coloured paper or paint can be added.

8. It is a good exercise in awareness and observation to set the class to find and copy textures in the room. These might include knitting, wood graining, hair, and many others. The range might be extended by means of a microscope.

9. Having made a 'collage' using a variety of materials such as beads, shiny paper, cloth and string, it is sometimes a good idea to copy this in colour so that the act of painting is clearly related to the actual textures of things.

10. The class might make 'contrast charts'. The aim would be to see how many pairs of contrasting materials could be assembled and mounted on cards. Here are suggestions: black, white; hard, soft; thick, thin; flexible, rigid; hot, cold; regular, irregular; plain, pattern; large, small; rough, smooth.

11. Experiments with pen and ink textures should include black with pin-points of white showing through. This gives a sparkle and prevents deadness. Various ways of doing a 'stipple' should also be tried. As this is one of the most difficult textures to produce successfully, the teacher should give a demonstration and emphasize, firstly, the need for an overall pattern of pen-strokes or brush-strokes that do not vary appreciably in size and, secondly, the gradation from black to white which will best be achieved by dividing the stipple into three areas; (a) solid black, (b) an area in which there are islands of white, and (c) an area of black shapes becoming more widely spaced.

12. A collage can be built up of materials such as stamps, labels, string and postal wrappings. Everyday material of this kind is easily obtained and yet if creatively used it can provide a fresh impact of visual awareness. The marks and symbols of our day-to-day lives are just as significant to us, and therefore of interest, as are the symbols of the mathematician to the scientist.

13. A composition can be created, using charcoal, Indian ink, and pasted newspaper. There is a similarity of texture between the broken quality of the newsprint and the vibrant line of the charcoal. The dense black ink provides a sharp contrast.

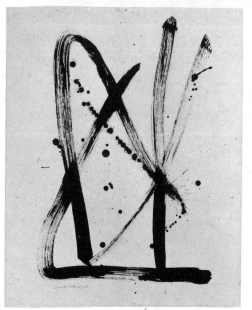

PLATE 25 Intuitive images. Girls age 13.

14. Old, worn wrapping-paper, strips of weather-beaten posters torn from billboards, discarded pieces of old leather – in short the outworn rubble of our day – can be collected. With suitable treatment, and used creatively, these items can provide compositions which appeal powerfully to the imagination, suggesting, for example, the forms of an eroded landscape.

15. Photographic material, either negative film or old discarded black and white photographs, can be used in designs of cut pieces that show effects not obtainable in any other way. Film ranges from dense black to clear transparency and portions of photographs can be selected that show good tonal and textural contrast.

16. A 'mosaic' design can be built up using a plastic paste-spreader. The colour should be thick and the squares placed as close as possible. The success of the design will depend on strong tonal contrasts to separate one area of the design from another, with subtle colour variations in each area. Once the method is understood it becomes possible to use mosaic materials – $\frac{1}{2}$ in. squares cut from leather-hard clay, decorated with coloured slip and fired in the school kiln. If this is not possible, pieces of square cut linoleum or small pebbles of similar size can be used. The mosaic pieces are glued on to a base and the spaces between filled with grout such as fine white cement or 'Polyfilla'.

Chapter 11

Three-dimensional art

Throughout the Basic Course the teacher will be wise to provide opportunities for students to work experimentally in three dimensions in a manner corresponding to their work in two dimensions. This will involve the handling of tools and a variety of materials, and the question of craftsmanship assumes some importance, but the teacher must see that the young student is not deterred by technical difficulties. The nature of the constructional work undertaken will depend partly on the skill and interest of the teacher and partly on the age of the students and their experience in handling tools. This chapter will attempt to indicate some work that is well within the capability of an 11- or 12-year-old boy or girl in the secondary school. At the same time suggestions will be made for further study involving equipment and materials in which more skill is required. There is not space in this chapter to go into full technical details, but the teacher in difficulty should consult some of the books listed in the bibliography. The drawings in Plates 26, 27, 28 and 29 are based on students' work (ages 11–17).

The question of craftsmanship is a matter about which a sense of proportion has to be kept. Students will gain little satisfaction from a construction which they feel 'does not work'; on the other hand, valuable aesthetic experience can be gained from experimental work which may not be up to the highest standards of craftsmanship. It should be remembered that the craftsman works from a preconceived idea which enables him to make the right technical approach, whereas the artist maintains his creative inspiration through all stages of his work, developing and maybe making changes that further his end. This is true not only of modelling, carving and constructions, but also of painting (and drawing). But whereas anyone can paint (in the sense at least of making paint stick to a surface) it is a different matter to make something out of wood or to cast a clay model. It is essential that the student should regard work in three dimensions as a further opportunity for individual imagination and initiative and that any technical knowledge should be a means to this end and not an end in itself.

The student must learn to understand the physical nature of the materials themselves in relationship to the basic laws of design. Hence it is important for the teacher to provide as wide a range of materials as possible so that students can learn to appreciate the expressive potentialities of each. This chapter deals with a number of inexpensive materials that have been found useful in the secondary school but it would be wise not to limit the students' experience to these only. From time to time opportunity should be made to experiment with unusual and new materials. This will give freshness and vitality to the work.

Hardboard or plywood is fairly easy to cut into square shapes, using a metal-backed tenon-saw, a trysquare and a sawing bench-hook. The edges can be made true with a glasspaper block. The pieces can be fixed together with glue and panel pins and fastened on to a baseboard. Rectangular division can be worked out in many different ways as shown in Plate 26. Sometimes the square pieces can be fixed into position with a thickness piece so that they project slightly from the baseboard to cast a shadow. Curved shapes can be cut with a coping-saw using a cutting-table and clamp or a carpenter's vice.

When the work is finished it should be coated with a white matt paint – e.g. a plastic-based white, or an oil-bound distemper. Matt white is normally a good colour to finish any three-dimensional work, since it takes the light well, but sometimes by way of contrast or to emphasize a centre of interest black or some primary colour may be used. The reason why primary colours are suggested, is that they are normally associated in the mind with strong square shapes – more subtle shapes such as are found in pottery might call for a more delicate sense of colour. Care should be taken that a dark colour does not obscure any shadows.

Plaster is an easier material in which to work. It requires fewer tools than hardboard. The plaster can be cast into slabs (size approximately 18 in. × 24 in. and about $\frac{1}{4}$ in. in thickness) by using some flat sheets of tin surrounded by a wooden frame to act as a wall. Any gaps between the wood and the tin can be sealed with clay before pouring in the liquid plaster. The tin should be lightly greased to prevent the plaster sticking to it. When set, and taken out of the frame, the plaster is easily cut by making a straight line with a sharp point drawn along a straight-edge and then snapping the plaster by pressing it firmly along the back of this line on the edge of a table.

A first exercise might consist of arranging, say, three rectangular shapes of different sizes and fixing them flat on a plaster base. The plaster is then soaked in water until it stops bubbling. The pieces are fixed using liquid plaster, which can conveniently be made in small quantities by putting a pinch of fresh

CONSTRUCTIONS using sheet material

(*below*) Use of plywood.

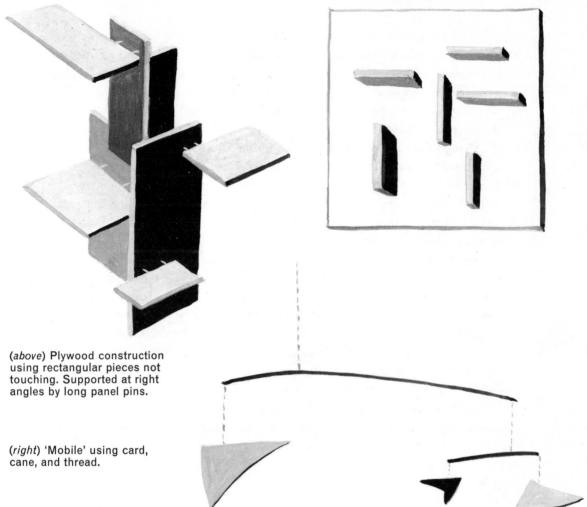

(*above*) Plywood construction using rectangular pieces not touching. Supported at right angles by long panel pins.

(*right*) 'Mobile' using card, cane, and thread.

(*left*) Contrasts of three curved shapes. Carved from sheet plaster and set at a distance from a plaster base.

PLATE 26

plaster into a teaspoon of water. It is not necessary to stir the mixture. The plaster can be applied with a pen-knife or with a small paste-brush. (Holes or broken corners can be repaired in the same way.) When set, the plaster can be smoothed with sandpaper. This work can be developed in the following ways:

(*a*) By using curved shapes. More unity might be obtained if it is suggested that the shapes be based on a free rendering of a letter of the alphabet (e.g. 'P', though the middle of the 'P' need not necessarily be removed). Curved shapes will require careful work with a pen-knife or a plaster-rasp.

(*b*) A rectangular shape can be set up at right angles to the base. Greater unity would be secured by using pieces of the same size throughout, e.g. squares. Interest would then be achieved by variation in spacing. Pieces of different thickness and proportion would give greater variety.

(*c*) Plaster can also be used in a freer manner, to build up compositions in three dimensions that are more intuitive in conception. These may bear some relationship to the principles of growth in natural things. The method is to assemble quantities of a common unit which might be, say, rectangular or pointed pieces, and to join these together with thin plaster. There is no pre-conceived arrangement, but rather the student works intuitively, building up the assemblage stage by stage in relationship to what has been done before. The common unit helps the unity of the whole.

The methods described so far are all building up, modelling, or construction processes. The method is one of *addition*. But the student should also gain experience of carving, that is of *subtraction*. For this purpose plaster will be required in large blocks. These can be cast in old cardboard boxes which can usually be provided by members of the class.

When the plaster is set, the first job is to square up the surfaces, using for this purpose an inexpensive 1-in. wood-working chisel. This is worked in different directions until the surface is quite level. It will be found that the straight sides of the blade are just as useful, if not more useful, than the sharpened end. A stiff, straight-bladed table-knife might be a useful substitute. This squaring up can be done by eye and it serves as a useful introduction to the use of the tool.

When this first stage has been satisfactorily completed the teacher should explain that the aim is to carve the plaster into a series of rectangular blocks to form an interesting arrangement. Each plane surface will be parallel to the original surfaces of the block, of simple rectangular shape but of varying sizes and proportions. It should be noted that sometimes the surfaces will be 'L' shaped but the aim of rectangular blocks must be held firmly in mind.

EXAMPLES OF PLASTER CARVING
(*below*) Design using simple rectangular forms.

(*top right*) Curved surfaces with contrasting circle.

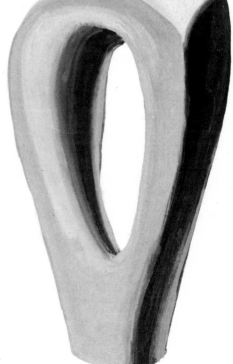

(*above*) A more completely realized curved form.
(*right*) A more complex shape involving a wire armature.

PLATE 27

It will be found necessary to supervise the work closely, otherwise the student may get into a complicated muddle, which is difficult to put right. For this reason it is advisable that each student should report when he has finished one particular stage of the work and seek permission before starting on another section. This is not so that the teacher should interfere with the creative process that is taking place, but rather that he should be sure that the student is conscientiously tackling his problem, which in the early stages has to be faced section by section. He must not evade the problem by thoughtlessly jumping from place to place.

A second exercise in plaster-carving would be the making of a simple curved shape using any irregular or broken pieces of plaster. Here the aim would be to achieve curves of constantly varying section. By way of contrast, one or more sharp edges could be introduced if desired. The chisel can also be used for curved shapes though one or two specially made plaster-working tools are a useful supplement (supplied by Messrs John Tiranti Ltd, 72 Charlotte Street, London W1). The final smoothness can be achieved with fine glasspaper. An important practical point is to see that the chisels are cleaned *and oiled* at the end of each lesson; because plaster readily causes rust.

Clay-modelling is a very useful means of developing a sense of volume and mass. Its plasticity and cheapness give it a place of special importance in the art room. Its difficulty is twofold. Firstly, the facility of manipulation leads easily to the modelling of tired and insipid forms. Secondly, since the student is usually interested in retaining the finished product, clay-modelling has to be cast into a more permanent material such as plaster (or fired as a terra-cotta). When the model is to be cast the method recommended is to use the clay in pellet form so that a sense of 'building up' the shape is achieved rather like using bricks. For this purpose the clay is used in rolls (about $\frac{1}{4}$–$\frac{1}{2}$ in. thick) and applied either with the fingers, or by means of a flat wooden or metal tool. The clay is used on a baseboard and everywhere is kept of substantial thickness (at least $\frac{1}{2}$ in.) so that it can be successfully cast into plaster. At first the pellets are applied in large pieces, then smaller pieces are fitted in between until the final surface is achieved. The aim is not to achieve a perfectly smooth finish which would appear dead and mechanical, but rather a lively sense of purpose and careful placing. The first exercise can be concerned with rectangular structure along the lines already suggested in connexion with plaster-carving, to be followed by curvilinear structure and rhythm.

Cardboard-modelling, using squared pieces of extra thick ivory card, can be

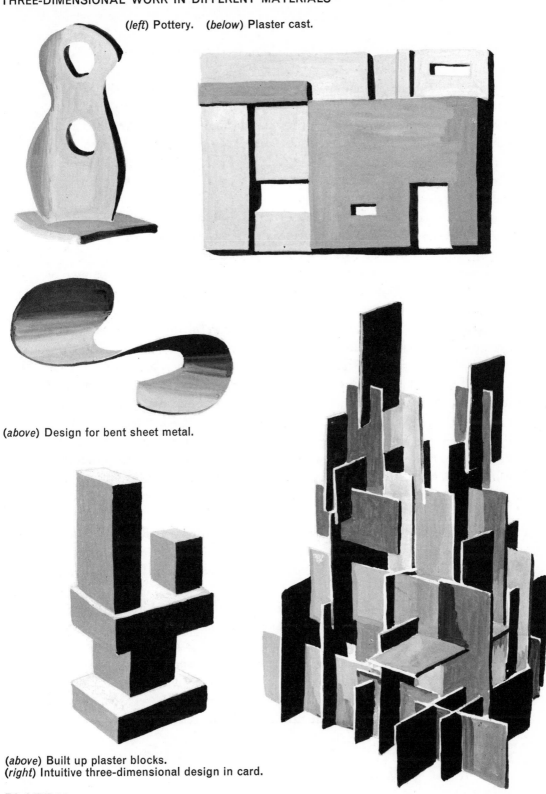

(*left*) Pottery.   (*below*) Plaster cast.

(*above*) Design for bent sheet metal.

(*above*) Built up plaster blocks.
(*right*) Intuitive three-dimensional design in card.

PLATE 28

used for experiments in rectangular division in three dimensions, and for the intuitive free building similar to that described earlier with plaster. The jointing can be done by cutting slots (with sufficient clearance to allow for the thickness of the material) so that the planes can penetrate each other. Everything is held firmly in place by strips of ½-in. bookbinding tape folded longways and pasted (with a preparation such as 'Gloy') on either side of each joint. Designs can be worked out using strips of card that have been bent into circles, segments of circles, scrolls, spirals or 'S' shapes and combined for contrast with straight pieces.

A practical consideration that has to be taken into account with all work in three dimensions is how the work will stand or be supported. In some cases a base of some sort may be required, but in general the aim should be to let the work be free-standing. Work can often be well displayed on a white-painted or white-covered bench near to a window. A display cabinet is very desirable as this protects the work from dust and finger marks.

The making of 'mobiles' is an activity well within the range of any secondary school class. It need not involve any materials other than thick ivory card, pins, thread, and pieces of cane or wire. Mobiles are a new art form that have a close relationship to drawing and painting with the added attraction of movement. The wire or canes are lines in space, while the shapes are each surrounded by light and space, each to some extent independent but related through balance, form and colour. The problem is one of relationship, and a first exercise could consist of balancing three straight-sided shapes so that they exhibit both harmony and contrast. A second mobile could consist of, say, five pieces of cardboard cut to curved shapes. The procedure for making mobiles is as follows:

(a) Mark the outlines of the shapes required on cardboard, aiming at a spontaneous and lively personal quality in the drawing. It does not matter if several lines are put one on top of the other. Cut out the final shapes with scissors.

(b) Suspend the two smallest shapes forming the lowest unit in the mobile by thread from the ends of a piece of cane about 6 in. long. Advantage should be taken of the natural curve of the cane. This is customary in mobiles, curved lines being more graceful than straight ones and giving a more satisfactory balance. (Wire, 14–16 gauge, can be used instead, but it is more difficult to manipulate.) The attachment to the cardboard is by means of a small pin tied to the thread and pushed into the top edge of each cardboard shape. The thread is joined to the cane by cutting a slight groove near the end of the cane and tying and glueing (with 'Seccotine').

(c) The next step is to make a temporary attachment to the cane with thread to find the point of balance before fixing the thread permanently. (This will not be in the middle of the cane, but nearer to the heavier shape.)

(d) This thread is, in turn, attached to the end of a second length of cane which must be longer than the first. The third shape is attached to the other end. This process can be continued until the required number of units are completed.

(e) With the completed mobile hung at a convenient height, the shapes and, if desired, the cane, can be painted with poster-colour. Black could be used for the shapes and white for the arms; or one of the shapes could be picked out in another colour.

Line-work in three dimensions can be easily practised using thick and thin pieces of cane, the two ends being supported by pushing them into holes bored in a piece of wood. If necessary, the cane can be softened by soaking in water so that it will bend as required without breaking. Cane can be bent sharply at right angles if first nipped at the bending-point with round-nosed pliers.

This chapter is longer than any other because this is a most important section of the Course and one which is neglected in many schools. The aim is twofold: (a) to give the student the opportunity of handling a wide variety of materials – in this respect this chapter overlaps that dealing with textures, and (b) to provide an opportunity of exploring form both in the classical sense of a relationship of parts to the whole and to each other, and also in the intuitive sense – informal arrangements which nevertheless give us a direct sense of pleasure, even if it is one difficult to define.

This exploration of form can be further divided into two main categories – that concerned with volume and mass (this is mostly the work of modelling and carving) and that concerned with spatial relationships (by means of construction). It should be remembered that modern techniques in architectural and engineering practice have enormously extended the possibilities of three-dimensional design and it is important educationally to develop and extend our awareness in this direction.

Suggestions for further study and experiment

1. Line work can be carried out in three dimensions by using copper wire which is bent as required with pliers. The two ends can be soldered together or inserted into a piece of wood. The size of the construction should not be too big, or it will lack firmness and stability and will look weak and ineffective.

2. Work on a larger scale can be carried out using wooden dowel-rod. One or more uprights can be fixed into a $\frac{3}{4}$-in. plywood base and horizontal pieces of varied length glued into sockets bored into the uprights at different intervals.

3. Rectangular constructions can be made using thin plywood and supporting the planes at right angles to each other by means of extra long panel pins. This opens up the design and increases the spatial effect so that there is a clear space between each piece of wood.

4. If pottery is practised as a school craft, a basic scheme of work can be devised in other ways; 'leather-hard' slabs of clay can be cut, pierced, bent and joined with slip. The fact that clay can so easily be cut and bent makes it a very useful medium for experimenting with curved shapes and curved surfaces. It will be found helpful in organizing the class to keep ready a supply of clay slabs in 'leather-hard' condition. If each student prepares a slab of clay for the 'bank' he can receive in exchange a piece in the right condition for immediate use. More complex forms could be built up from thrown shapes.

5. Experiments can be carried out with bent sheet metal such as copper. Ideas can be tried out with cut paper or card.

6. Perspex, plain or coloured, can be used in various ways. Thus a simple black curvilinear shape can be cut out and fixed, by means of a thickness piece, a slight distance in front of a contrasting white rectangular surface.

7. Interesting work can be made from a plaster cast. First, a collection of pieces of balsa wood of varied shape are well soaked in clay-water so that they swell and are coated with a thin layer of clay. These are arranged on a base-board. Four strips of wood or glass are fixed to form the edge. Liquid plaster is run in to form the mould which is used as the finished piece of work. The mould will need reinforcing with pieces of thick wire and more plaster before it is removed from the board. The pieces of wood can more easily be removed when dry.

8. Hollow shapes can be made using an armature of wire or expanded metal covered either with *papier mâché* or plaster of Paris. The latter is splashed over all surfaces until the overall thickness is more than sufficient and is then carved and smoothed to the final surface.

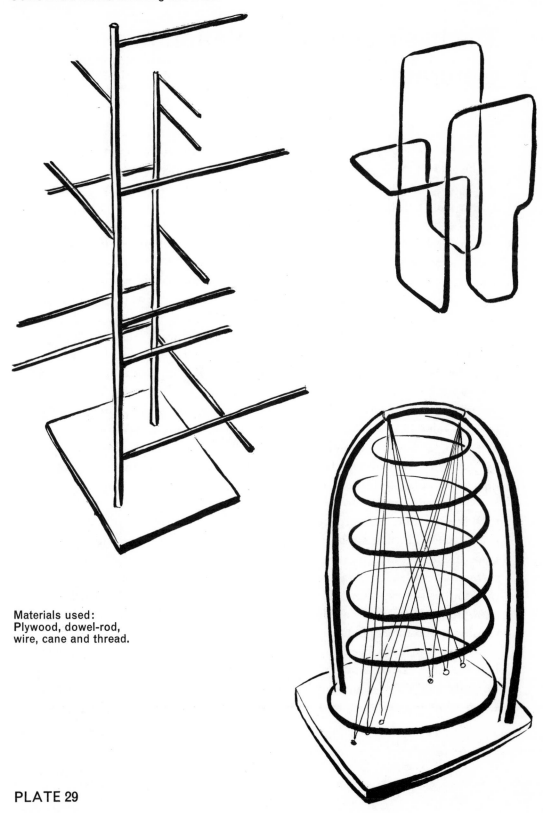

Materials used:
Plywood, dowel-rod,
wire, cane and thread.

PLATE 29

Chapter 12

The basic course in relation to picture-making

The intention throughout the Basic Course has been that the suggestions given at the end of each chapter should, through personal discovery, encourage development into creative art, showing good contrasts of shape, tone, line or colour. This will be increasingly possible as the work proceeds and different aspects of the Basic Course are combined together. It has been emphasized, too, in the Introduction that gifted students specially interested in figurative work should be given plenty of opportunity to pursue their special interests alongside the work on the Basic Course. This was suggested because it is most important for the teacher in the secondary school to preserve the opportunity for all aspects of personal expression. Care must be taken to avoid making the Basic Course a forcing-house for abstract or non-objective art. Under wise guidance the most profuse output of original and unsophisticated work takes place in the later years of the primary school. But all too soon the young adolescent becomes aware of adult standards and he is tempted to copy the second-rate in the world around him. This is where the Basic Course can be of especial value in providing a line of development for the creative urge. It will also help to establish confidence which will provide a basis for the further development of creative picture-making. This chapter will attempt to suggest some ways in which this can be done.

Experiments can be worked out with circles. Using cardboard milk-bottle tops or something similar, four circles can be drawn, irregularly spaced on white paper. The first circle can be defined by shading the edge with grey and black inside the line, the second by shading outside the line, the third can be surrounded with a flat black colour, and the fourth can be solid black. Such questions as the following will then present themselves – does the black circle on white look the same as the white circle on black? What is the effect of shading inside the edge of a circle and outside the edge?

We are now ready to explore further. A piece of white paper can be divided into two unequal parts by an horizon line. The aim is to paint each half in a carefully modulated colour which is a pale tint at the horizon and a dark shade at the top and bottom. Complementary colours can be used, e.g. yellow

PLATE 30 'The Escape' – painting by a girl of 17.

and violet-blue. It is best to start with white, then gradually to add increasing quantities of colour, using long horizontal strokes, and finally to darken still more by adding increasing quantities of black. The effect of recession that has been achieved can then be augmented by painting in line only (using black or white, or both) three (or more) objects that are arranged so as to give an effect of diminishing height or size. The following objects are suggested: figures, telegraph-poles, columns, birds, or objects connected with space exploration.

A composition can be based on rectangular shapes and equilateral or similar triangles to suggest a town or village scene. This can be worked out on large sheets of grey paper using shapes of black and white paper arranged to fill the picture-space with an interesting variety of roofs, walls and windows. It is better to concentrate on shapes and their relationship rather than on lines and tricks of perspective. As far as possible the general directions should be vertical and horizontal, in harmony with the frame. When the basic relationships are established some pupils might wish to add contrasting linear shapes in the form of trees, or curved shapes in the form of hills or people. Others might wish to examine the possibilities of making the picture into a harbour scene with the tall, narrow, triangular sails of yachts.

Another composition can be based on curved lines. Take a large sheet of grey paper. Draw in charcoal 'a winter tree' sufficiently big for the lines to reach to the edge of the paper. The drawing might be based on a view of trees seen from the art-room windows or carefully drawn sketches made out of doors. If this is not possible some small branches could be supported by 'Plasticine' to suggest trees. It is important that the teacher should see that every line is placed with thought and care. 'Branching out' and 'crossing' relation-ships should be vigorous, and the spaces between lines should show contrasting and varied shapes. Special attention should be paid to the base of the tree and its relationship to the ground. White, black, and grey colours could be used for the tree and varied cool blue-grey colours for the spaces between the branches.

The same approach can be used for 'a summer tree'. This time the branches can be painted with a brush in black and the spaces between can be painted in varied greens – warm and cool, light and dark.

The space at the bottom of the picture can be filled with a landscape of buildings or fields. Alternatively, people or animals can be drawn under the tree. In adding these subsidiary features it is important to keep a simple treatment in harmony with the rest of the picture – trying to avoid any tricky

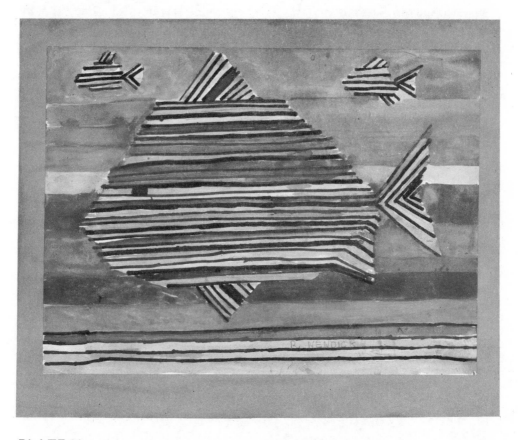

PLATE 31 (*top*) Linocut based on triangle relationships. Girl age 17.
(*bottom*) 'Fishes' – line and point design. Boy age 12.

perspective effects or details which do not accord with the general relationships.

Some pictures can be painted using only white paint on black paper. This is an excellent preparation for lino-block design and it helps to concentrate attention on the need for rhythmical lines and shapes. Large bird-, fish-, animal-, and flower-forms can be rendered in this manner. Alternatively, work can be done on white paper using graphite sticks or cheap black oil-paint (decorators' or students' colour in tubes). Here the aim is to develop the student's ability by providing media which allow him to record his ideas with ease and rapidity. Large quantities of the cheapest paper should be provided. The method is as follows. First, place some black paint on a palette or small plate. Dip a large flat bristle- or paste-brush in turps substitute and then press one corner of the brush into the paint. Hold the brush well up and use large free swinging strokes. If the paint is applied to only one corner of the brush a shaded line will be produced. The graphite stick held in the fingers can be employed in the same way by using the square end and applying more pressure to one edge.

Very often, when inexperienced students tackle pictorial work, they think of the main subject of the picture as distinct from the background, with the result that the picture lacks harmony. It is important therefore that they should learn to think of the picture as a whole. All the shapes and spatial relationships require equal thought and care. Every part of the picture must be seen in relationship to the focal point or to the total design.

Another difficulty with inexperienced students concerns the use of colour. Too often there is only a slavish copying of 'local colour' which will result in a lack of harmony in the picture. The aim, once again, is to conceive the picture as a whole – this time in terms of colour.

The teacher is reminded that the suggestions at the end of each chapter are not to be presented as a set of routine exercises such as one might find in a book of arithmetic. Rather are they to be interpreted as possible lines of development in which the student can experience the joy of creative adventure. This is especially important in picture-making. Although the initial exercises set out in this chapter may need to be conscious to meet the needs of some students, it should always be remembered that the aim is to develop the intuitive sensibility. There is a danger that the approach to picture-making can be over-systematized. Hence it is suggested that each of the subjects that follow might be treated in one of several ways according to the needs of a particular class:

PLATE 32

(*top*) 'Houses' – a palette-knife painting showing good tone contrasts. Based on simple area division avoiding the use of line. Girl age 13.

(*bottom left*) Painting of bonfire, showing rich textural quality.

(*bottom right*) 'Still life' showing contrasts of curved and straight-sided shapes with dotted lines. Boy age 13.

(*a*) The proposed subject might be discussed and suggestions put forward by members of the class as to how it might be treated in terms of colour, shape, line and tone.

(*b*) The interpretation of the subject or proposed method of working might be left entirely to the class, and suggestions made only when asked for in individual cases.

(*c*) Ideas could first be rapidly worked out in charcoal and possibly samples of the principal colours might be mixed. These could then be compared and discussed before the actual painting commences.

Suggestions for further work

1. Yachting pictures give an opportunity to explore triangle relationships. These can be worked out in line and then painted in a limited number of carefully chosen colours.

2. Underwater scenes give scope for exploring the relationships of free-flowing curved forms.

3. 'Still life' pictures can be worked out by drawing contrasted shapes (such as an apple and a mug, or a coffee-pot and a vase) related either to straight or curved lines which divide up the picture-space.

4. 'Picture-making from objects' – a picture can be created using an assembly of shapes seen in the room (or from sketches made elsewhere). Thus a chair might be used as the main subject, not as the basis of a naturalistic study, but rather using, for example, the positive form of the shape of the seat or the negative forms created by the spaces between the rails and the uprights. Shapes suggested by imagined objects can be added as desired.

5. Pictures can be based on an imaginative development of 'scribbled', 'smudged', or other partly accidental effects.

6. Creative compositions can be carried out by 'photo-montage'. One or more photographic reproductions of people or objects can be cut out of a magazine, arranged and pasted on to paper and combined, if desired, with abstract shapes. This method gives an excellent opportunity of creating 'dream' pictures containing an unusual juxtaposition of objects or parts of the figures. The irrational and absurd will find a ready response in any class, and the use of reproductions helps those who find drawing difficult. The whole composition must be linked and harmonized by painting.

7. Heads of figures or animals can be drawn as near-abstract compositions.

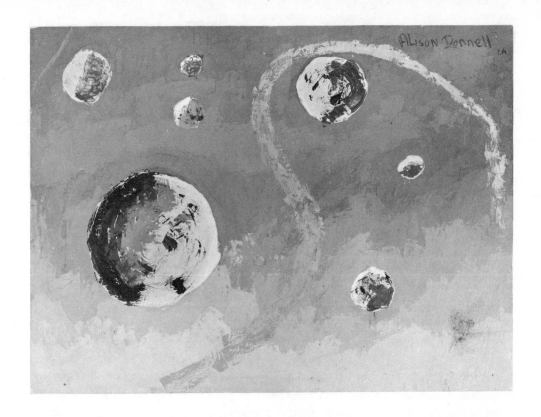

PLATE 33 (*top*) 'Planets in space' – based on point design with curved line and varied tone added to enhance the spatial quality. Girl age 13.
(*bottom*) 'Pony in a snowstorm' – rhythmic use of curves. Girl age 13.

Any details such as 'hair' or 'eye' will influence the design and should only be used (if at all) with thoughtful care. Finish with paint to give a variety of textures. If students find it difficult to abstract from something so close to their experience, the head could first be worked out with materials such as string, matches and buttons.

8. Imaginative painting can be stimulated by models. Thus a small setting could be created (older students might make their own) using mirrors, string, textured materials, and objects, to be interpreted by the students in different ways.

9. A colour can be chosen for a monochromatic picture. This picture can then be based on the association brought to mind by the chosen colour. Thus 'red' might suggest a fire, a street, or Hell! As far as possible the picture should be painted using only this colour in all its variations plus the neutral colours. Then with permission another chosen colour could be used.

10. The theme 'planets in space' can be started as a point design based on contrasted sizes and then painted to create effects of nearness or distance by means of tone and colour relationships. The graduated colour must be applied not only to the main subject of the picture but to the whole area so as to enhance the full spatial quality.

11. A straight-line composition based on horizontal and vertical line relationships can be developed as a 'view through scaffolding'. A few converging lines could be used to suggest depth but care should be taken not to lose the creative aspect of the composition through a technical concern with formal perspective. Or a theme based on Paul Klee's 'transparent cubes seen in perspective' can be worked out.

12. A 'fish' design can be worked out in black line (like an X-ray photograph in reverse). Use a main horizontal axis represented by one, two, or more lines and, from this, lines can project on both sides. The projecting lines can vary in length, distance apart, or thickness. They can be straight or curved. Further lines at an angle for fins and tail could be added if necessary.

Fill in the spaces between the lines with variations of one colour. If desired, the eye could be suggested with a touch of brighter colour. Use a contrasting colour with some variations for the surrounding space.

An alternative subject suitable for this treatment would be a tree, using a vertical axis.

PLATE 34 (*left*) 'Winter tree' – a free intuitive approach. Girl age 14.
(*right*) 'Head' – a linear design using wool, string, and buttons. Note the way the
profile and full face are suggested in the drawing. Boy age 14.

Chapter 13

The importance of art in modern education

The teacher should look for opportunities to show how such things as colour sense and awareness of space affect our daily living; e.g. in the home, in the school buildings, in town planning. Two empty rooms of equal size can have vastly different effects. The room which will appear to have the most space will be the one with the simplest forms – one large window instead of three or four smaller ones, unbroken wall- and ceiling-surfaces and flush doors. The main effect in any room will always depend upon proportion and the careful placing of doors and window areas, but good proportions can be altered and spoilt by unsuitable colour. On the other hand, colour can help to retrieve a badly proportioned room, and best of all, of course, it can enhance a room of good proportions.

Domestic architecture is to be thought of in terms not so much of walls and roof as of the space to be lived in. Inside the home we should be aware of sensations of spaciousness, and of cosiness – of comfort and elegance – of cheerfulness and relaxation. These paired opposites are not always easy to reconcile but the success of the home atmosphere depends on the unification of these diverse qualities. Only a sound art training will provide the possibility of solving so teasing a problem.

Spatial relationships are even more important outside the home than in, since posterity will suffer for our lack of foresight and planning. Houses built in parallel rows are less pleasant to live in than houses grouped and facing each other across friendly greens. Modern town planning is having to deal more seriously with such problems as pedestrian precincts, underground or covered car parks, shopping areas, and the like, but more important still is the sort of positive planning that makes the inhabitants proud to live in certain communities – towns planned for light and air and good living: a combination of concentration and openness – a sufficiency of trees and grass to emphasize the urbanity by contrast – tall buildings closing vistas and contrasting with low ones – open spaces that are well planned and well used, not pieces left over from a jigsaw-puzzle that did not quite work out.

All this visible order in the town is important just because it can be seen. On the other hand an appreciation of the functional perfection, e.g. the sewage disposal system, can rouse little or no response. An architecturally ordered town is the symbol of an ordered society and is itself a stimulus to further cooperation. But the citizen will have that kind of visual awareness that demands better things only if he has had an education which has developed his capacity to respond to his environment, an education that is related to everyday life. This is where study of the history of architecture can be such a rewarding experience, presented not as so many 'styles' but from the point of view of appreciation of structure, form and spatial relationships.

The teacher should also make the student aware of the contribution of the modern artist to daily living. We owe much to the work of men like Mondrian who helped to forge a basic language of design. By 1917 he was no longer abstracting from nature as so many of his contemporaries were doing, but was using the simplest possible shapes and colours to build up his design from within. He was the foremost of a group of young Dutch architects and painters who were responsible for creating a common language for painting, sculpture, and architecture.

At first through the publication of the magazine called *De Stijl* (Style), and later through the foundation of the Bauhaus under Gropius (first at Weimar, then at Dessau), these ideas had a tremendous influence not only on architecture but also on every kind of industrial design. Art was no longer thought of as superficial ornament but as a very necessary part of everyday life. If art is no longer ornament, then form, line and colour can convey meaning and have an emotional impact. The television receiver, or the refrigerator, can convey a feeling of inert clumsiness or of grace and efficiency.

If we are willing to concede that form can be satisfying in itself it introduces us to new realms of experience. Kandinsky creates movement and excitement in his painting like the sounds of music. Nervous lines and amorphous shapes give his painting a very different quality from the austere perfection of Mondrian or Ben Nicholson. It will be obvious that work on the Basic Course will lead the student to an understanding of contemporary painting.

The student should also be encouraged to approach the work of school crafts with a more lively imagination. For instance, lettering becomes something more than mere copying if the reasons for the different letter forms are understood. The letter 'E' is a relationship of a vertical line and horizontal lines. As a piece of geometry with equal spaces and horizontals of equal length it may be regarded as having an elemental emotional appeal. In this form it would best harmonize with a letter 'C' or 'S' drawn geometrically. More subtlety can be introduced by varying the spaces and the lengths of the horizontal strokes.

Pottery is an especially valuable school craft for experiments with both two-dimensional and three-dimensional aspects of basic form relationships, together with the complementary qualities of colour, texture and pattern. Pottery can also be used for practical ends. Thus a handle can be thought of as a form of subtle variation, e.g. of line and section. But a handle has also to provide a firm grip, so it should look as though it is capable of doing this. The handle should appear to grow naturally out of the body and be strong enough to sustain the weight. It should bear a satisfying relationship with the form of the body of the pot. Pottery should never look like a collection of parts stuck together. A useful exercise for the student potter is, in fact, to join a series of parts together – these could consist of some cylinder forms of similar diameter with flanges (made as a part of 'throwing' practice) – and then to 'turn' them so that the vessel has an entity which exhibits both variation and unity. The glazing of a pot accentuates the form by throwing the light and shade into emphatic zones of light and dark. This shading can emphasize and enhance the main features of the pot. The colour and texture of the glaze can increase the emotional effect.

If decoration is scratched (*Sgraffito*) in the coloured slips, or painted in under-glaze colours in abstract designs, the student will have an excellent opportunity of using the knowledge gained on the Basic Course. The tendency to use floral patterns should be resisted as it leads to pretty effects, the copying of second-hand ideas and a turning aside from the basic problems. Pottery is an abstract art like music, for it is the contemplation of lines and masses, rhythm, harmony and movement which is the source of aesthetic pleasure.

As well as practical work, time should be given to looking at, and discussing, the design of everyday things such as furniture, glass, dress and motor-cars. Where possible, the actual objects can be displayed in a well-lighted showcase in some central part of the school. Local firms of high repute for the quality of their merchandise might be asked to set up attractive displays for short periods – which they are often willing to do without charge. Photographs and cuttings from magazines can also be displayed in some central position – usually under special headings to form wall exhibitions. These can be changed at least twice a term. A wall newspaper which can be changed weekly will give news of new buildings, town planning, and sometimes items of local interest. All these things bring contemporary ideas about art before students who may have dropped practical art and craft subjects.

PLATE 35   Painting based on an industrial theme. Girl age 17.

Play production offers a good opportunity for cooperation between art and craft teachers and those of other subjects and helps to establish the importance of art in the life of the school. Often the type of work done in the Basic Course can be directly related to theatrical requirements. Thus the production of T. S. Eliot's *Murder in the Cathedral* requires the atmosphère of a cathedral. It is hardly possible to create this on a normal school stage by conventional methods without a sham effect, but large abstract paintings based on a predominance of upright lines together with a variety of recessive blues, black-and-white and some pure and broken red will symbolize the vertical soaring lines of a cathedral broken by shafts of light and the glowing colour of stained glass.

Most arts, such as painting, poetry and sculpture, can be practised by 'individuals'. The nature of theatre art is different. It is composite, being made up of many arts fused together – lighting, costume, painting, music – and also communal because individuals must work together with a common understanding and purpose. Without this common vision the acting, design, lighting cannot come together – they will only exist each as an end in itself. The work of a producer is similar to that of an architect – he too has to coordinate the work of many experts to fulfil the particular requirements of the whole.

In all these things the student should remember that a work of art must produce one dominating effect although it is composed of many parts. Its form is the result of these parts being brought into harmonious relationship, into scale and proportion with one another, and with the whole.

Bibliography

CREATIVE CLAYWORK. *Harald Isenstein.* Oak Tree Press (London 1960).

MODELLING FOR AMATEURS. *Clifford and Rosemary Ellis.* Studio (London, 2nd rev. ed. 1945), o.p.

HOW TO MAKE MOBILES. *John Lynch.* Thames and Hudson (London 1953), o.p.

PATTERN AND TEXTURE. *J. A. Dunkin Wedd.* Studio (London 1956), o.p.

MOSAICS. *Doris and Diane Lee Aller.* Lane Book Co. (California 1960).

The five books above are among many that provide useful technical advice as well as creative ideas.

HOW TO MAKE COLLAGES. *John Lynch.* Thames and Hudson (London 1961).
A book full of ideas for picture-making and compositions involving textures.

ART FORMS IN NATURE. *Karl Blossfeldt.* Zwemmer (London 1935), o.p.
The 1953 German edition URFORMEN DER KUNST is, however, still available from Zwemmer.

PLANT MARVELS IN MINIATURE. *C. Postma.* Harrap (London 1960).
The two books above contain enlarged and magnified photographs of plants and plant structure.

ART NOW (new and enlarged edition). *Herbert Read.* Faber and Faber (London 1961).
A valuable book for presenting the theories that lie behind modern art.

CREATIVE CRAFTS IN EDUCATION. *Seonaid Robertson.* Routledge and Kegan Paul (London 1952).
A book which insists on the unity of art and crafts. Not a book on techniques but full of suggestions for creative activity.

ART SINCE 1945. Thames and Hudson (London 1959).
A symposium on the significance of abstract painting in our time. The illustrations in this and the two books which follow should give ideas for a Basic Course.

A CONCISE HISTORY OF MODERN PAINTING. *Herbert Read.* Thames and Hudson (London 1959).

A DICTIONARY OF ABSTRACT PAINTING. *Michel Seuphor.* Methuen (London 1957).

HENRY MOORE – SCULPTURE AND DRAWINGS. Volume One (1921–48), 4th revised edition.
Volume Two (Works since 1949). *Introductions by Herbert Read.* Lund Humphries (London 1957-8).

BARBARA HEPWORTH. *Introduction by J. P. Hodin.* Lund Humphries (London 1961).

BEN NICHOLSON. *John Summerson.* Penguin Modern Painter Series (London 1948).

KLEE: A STUDY OF HIS LIFE AND WORK. *G. Di San Lazzaro.* Thames and Hudson (London 1957).

THE MIND AND WORK OF PAUL KLEE. *Werner Haftmann.* Faber and Faber (London 1954).

The two books above are suggested since this artist, while a teacher at the Bauhaus in the 1920's, was responsible for pioneering work on basic design.

IMPRESSIONISM. *Peter de Francia.* FAUVISM. *Denis Mathews.* EXPRESSIONISM. *Edith Hoffmann.*
CUBISM. *Alfred Schmeller.* SURREALISM. *Alfred Schmeller.* ABSTRACT ART. *Frederick Gore.*
These inexpensive books have been found useful as sources of ideas and inspiration for use on the Basic Course. They appear in the series Movements in Modern Art, Methuen (London 1956).

FORM AND SPACE. *Eduard Trier.* Thames and Hudson (London 1961).

ART AND VISUAL PERCEPTION. *Rudolf Arnheim.* Faber and Faber (London 1956).
This book analyses basic design from a psychological point of view.

THE DEVELOPING PROCESS. Published by Kings College in the University of Durham on the occasion of an exhibition at the Institute of Contemporary Arts (London 1959), o.p.

MOTIF NOS. 8 AND 9. Shenval Press (London 1962).
A quarterly symposium which contains articles on basic design.

PHOTOVISION. *Roy Bethers.* Photography Magazine (London 1957), o.p.
Basic design applied to photography.

CREATIVE WOODCRAFT. *Ernst Röttger.* B. T. Batsford (London 1961).
This book shows how wood can be used to awaken the child's creative faculties along the lines of the Basic Course.